Producer and Publisher: Erik Fogg

Editor and Layout Designer: Steph Tyll

ISBN-13: 978-0-9898654-1-8

Contents

Intro. 2

Part I. Step-by-Step Guide to Reclaiming Your Time. 19

Acknowledgements

I'll keep these brief:

First and mostly thank you to mom, for carefully manicuring my education (in and outside the class) like a bonsai tree. None of this, including getting into MIT at all, would have happened without you. Thanks also for the funding, the excitement, and for sharing with all your mom-friends.

Thanks to my gramma and grampa, who support every nutty idea of mine as a matter of faith (and helped significantly with funding despite having no idea what an ebook is).

Thanks to Heather for lots of support and encouragement for an otherwise excessively harebrained scheme. I know I require a lot of patience and that this project was probably particularly demanding.

Thanks to Stephanie, who wore many hats to edit and publish this here book, and showed great patience along the way.

Thanks to other unnecessarily generous funders and friends who horked up cash and bought copies despite having graduated long ago, including: Andrew Farrell, Holly Fogg, Mark Daniels, Allison Matus, Ralph Caprio, Heather Pangle, Terral Jordan, Meghan Elledge, Arthur Petron, Moni Gallegos, Anton DeWinter, Sam Mohyee, Clint Lohse, Farhad Ghamsari, Michael Scott, Eric Han, Clif Dickens, Muhammad Qasim, Rick May, Brad Cook, Jason Gross, Mohamed Malik, Wagner P Dunin, Jack Fuge, son4ik, jtaylorapps, twiggernaut, Ned McNally, Joshua Karper, betta90210, jscuteri, renjamin, Mark Dobson, Anna Rady, lipkowitz, Jane Fogg, Mary Cole, Paige R., and Scott Garland.

PART 0
Intro

Foreword: Two All Nighters and a Freshman 20

It was freshman year (2005), fall term. I had the standard four-class workload, and I was absolutely drowning.

As I'm sure you're gleaning, I wasn't always the productivity rock star I brag of—certainly not at the beginning of college. I was a pretty smart kid and, sadly, never really learned to work hard in high school. MIT was a major kick in the pants that nearly knocked me flat.

Part of the problem was that I was taking Computer Science and I was just plain awful at it. (I'm still atrocious!) But most of the problem was that I had no idea how to work effectively. I'd be blissfully distracted and inefficient during the day and find myself starting my problem sets (or, as non-MIT'ers call it, "homework") at 10pm one or two nights before they were due.

The really bad news? Three of the four sets were due on Mondays. So Sunday night would roll around, and there I would be, only just getting started. On rare good weeks I'd been able to eke out some of the work beforehand. This was how many of my colleagues got through school, though, and I told myself that if I wanted them around for help, I'd have to work on their schedule. At the time, it was a very effective excuse for procrastinating; only later did I realize how badly I wasted my time during the week as I waited to get started on homework.

So there I was: it was early November and I was flat-out failing Computer Science (also known as 6.001). I'd gotten "used to" pulling all-nighters at that point, but we had midterms coming up – all packed, of course, into the same week... on top of regular problem being due. It was truly cruel.

On this particular Sunday night, I'd missed my opportunity for Friday night fun because I was working. I'd pulled an all-nighter Saturday night, and was now in the middle of my second. (For what it's worth, I'm lousy at all-nighters. I get tired, I get cranky, I usually give up halfway through, and I do more complaining than working.) But it was do-or-die for this Computer Science mid-term.

I was trying desperately to solve some tough problems as practice, but I felt myself fading. I cracked my twelfth Red Bull. At this point, I was jittery but no longer alert, so I went for a cold shower.

Before entering the shower, I looked at myself, towel-clad, in the mirror. I had dark, purplish bags under my eyes (that I've never quite gotten rid of since—they are like scars), a new, jiggly chin and a serious pair of love handles, flowing over the sides of the towel like a muffin—ugh. In just three months I'd put on over 20 lbs.

I broke down and cried in the bathroom. I hated my life and I hated what I'd become. Unsure of what to do (and too proud to use MIT's superb Student Support Services), I took a shower and tried to power through the rest of the night, tears making my notes run on the page. I trudged to the mid-term the next day like I was on a death march. And, as you'd predict, I failed it. I went home that day and fell into the oblivion of heavy sleep.

This was when I knew I had to either change things dramatically or give up. And change dramatically I did - if you didn't know me at the beginning, you'd think that I either was one of MIT's super-prodigies who coded in their sleep or that I worked myself to death to graduate. In the four years I was at MIT, I got a Bachelor's degree with two minors, a Master's, and learned Chinese. (I also managed to squeak by Computer Science with C minus minus minus, for all the good it did me!) While a few exceptional folks—all of whom had some combination of superior intellect and work ethic to my own—performed similar feats, doing this without the mega-brains or grueling sleep-deprivation was, largely speaking, unheard of.

So how'd I get to the end of yon tunnel?

I gut-checked after mid-terms were done and I'd caught up on sleep. Looking at myself again in the mirror, I saw in my eyes the man I wanted to be, swimming deep under the surface. As the first person in my family to go to university, I had a lot to prove. I wasn't willing to let myself quit, but I was (and still am) far too lazy to pull all-nighters and work myself to death. I vowed then never to pull an all-nighter again, and in the eight years since I never have (with the exception of a few really, really good parties!).

What I did then was build a system, albeit a sloppily cobbled-together one. Finally being honest with myself, I saw that I was wasting a ton of time during the week with procrastination and distraction by my (wonderful) friends. I was studying poorly—I put in a lot of time, but it wasn't effective. I started by sitting down and really determining what I wanted out of college. I flat-out dropped a half-dozen major commitments that weren't important to me (ruffling a few feathers along the way, but I don't regret it). I built a schedule, killed Facebook, and rooted out wasted time everywhere I could find it.

After months of tweaking my system, I had become a sleep glutton and an academic juggernaut. MIT students have a common saying: "school, sleep, social: pick two." Despite my natural weaknesses, I proved this a false constraint—I had all three.

I had so much time on my hands, I was able to give it back. I became scholarship chair at my fraternity, teaching the system to the freshmen (and some of the upperclassmen). I started sharing what I was doing over a beer with my friends. I can say proudly that everyone I worked with graduated on time and (probably) with a bit more sanity.

Today, my towel-clad all-nighter remains a haunting memory of near failure, and the bags under my eyes greet me every morning in the mirror. What's worse, not everyone I knew made it out of their own similar crashes—dozens of folks I know dropped out, switched schools, failed out, or took 9-12 semesters to finish their degree. These were smart, motivated, industrious MIT students. For many of them, their careers are shaken—for others, their spirits crushed. Some thought they "just couldn't cut it" at MIT, that they lacked inner talent or grit; but they took the wrong lessons away from their struggles. They didn't have the right structure on their side to crush college, and it's a goddamned tragedy: the world would be a better place had they recovered.

College, for *everyone*, is way too tough, way too expensive, and way too important for these stories to be the norm. But they are: 60% of American students entering college *won't graduate in four years*. Of them, 40% will not graduate within *six*. Consider: where will you fall in that pile of statistics?

I wrote this book because I decided I wasn't willing to sit back and let that keep happening. College *should* be stressful, but in a way that teaches you to work well, not to suffer. It should stretch you, but not break you. And it sure as hell shouldn't make you any more bankrupt than it plans to.

So this is my mission: I want *you* to get more sleep, have more fun, learn more, do more, get better grades with less work, graduate on time (or early!), and save a giant gob of money. I want you to take your life back and redirect your time to what's most important.

Time and again I have run into people that believe they just can't cut it or that they lack some innate skill. They see those who are highly productive as supermen, as something naturally apart from others. Time and again, they are amazed that the whole time they were missing just a few key, easily learned concepts and skills that changed the game.

Sadly, no level of education (at least in the US) teaches you how to use your time as effectively as you need to be able to, so it's no wonder that most people don't know how to do so by the time they get to college. But that's what you're going to learn here.

This isn't just about productivity: it's about thriving, rather than treading water. I want the simple methods that worked for me to become so ubiquitous in our national lexicon that people don't need to buy this guide anymore. I want to change the American university experience forever. In short, I want you (and every single other student out there) to Crush College.

Enjoy.

How to Get the Most Out of Crush College

There are a lot of names for a very important concept in life: the "moment of truth," the "revelation," the "burning platform." Tim Ferris calls it the "Harajuku moment." They all describe the moment when you decide you're really going to change, and with that decision form a deep internal motivation that sticks for months or years.

Change ain't easy. For me (as with many), it required total breakdown. Thus the "burning platform" concept: the present situation is so unacceptable that you're willing to "leap forth" into the unknown to change it. For some, this only requires the realization that life can be a whole lot better and more exciting.

Ultimately, **you** are the X-factor in Crush College (but you already knew this). What this means: to get the most out of this book, you need to commit. Not to many hours of work (that would be tragically ironic), but to changing your habits, to pushing yourself out of your comfort zone, and to hanging on when it gets scary.

This means having a very clear vision of *where you are now and where you want to be*. In order to have the willpower to persist through change, you must be able to see change happening. Crush College makes it easy to generate quick wins that will stick, but until you know what you want to do with your extra time—that is, where you want to be— you're just going to spend that new free time on Facebook, Youtube, or your phone.

We'll go over this in more detail in Chapter 1, "Creating Force-Ranked Goals," but know this: the most important thing you need to do to get the most out of this book is to paint a vivid picture for yourself of what your new life is going to be like. Put it down on paper: exactly how much sleep you'll get, what your social life will look like, what activities you want to pick up (cooking, the gym, etc), how you'll feel, and what your academic accomplishments will be. Where you're not sure, make it up, but be ambitious. This picture you've painted will be your reminder of why you're going through the change. (And if you don't want to change anything about your life: well, you're probably reading the wrong book!)

The second key to success for Crush College is to implement *one thing at a time*. It's tempting to try to change everything at once, but it won't work. You'll get overloaded, you won't be able to measure what's working and what's not, and you won't be able to tweak anything that's "in progress" to get it right… so a lot of your efforts will fail outright.

You wouldn't try to learn to swim, ride a bike, shoot a basketball, and do calculus all at once. Be patient.

Crush College is structured to build sequentially upon the parts before; I've ordered the guide such that the most important and impactful parts come earlier. If you read through a chapter and feel like you have a *really good* handle on it, go ahead and skip it, but make sure you read it first. There's some unorthodox stuff in here.

Finally: use data and trust your gut. I have recommended changes to make and have provided a number of tips, but they're meant to serve first as examples and second as inspiration. Ultimately, you will be learning a process to quickly develop the solutions that work best for you, rather than adopting those that worked for someone else, but may not be relevant to you. So be ready to put your thinking cap on. This is designed to be easy, but it does require you to be *engaged*, or you won't get anywhere.

Ready? Excellent.

What's Covered and What to Expect

All right, folks: we're going to keep this guide short and awesome. (Like Tyrion Lannister.) I've condensed the material as much as possible while keeping it clear. No fluff. There are three Parts (plus an intro and closing) that each cover a different aspect of the overall Crush College system.

Before we dive in, we'll review the **principles**. These are the concepts you're going to keep in your mind and apply to everything you do until it becomes automatic. If you forget everything else and internalize these, you'll be able to re-derive most of the rest of the process. Know them. Love them. Repeat them at night to help you fall asleep.

In Part I, we're going to cover a **process** that quickly takes you from your "burning platform" to your paradise island of productivity, satisfaction, and freedom. Each chapter will take you step-by-step through conquering the challenges in college life that destroy your time and keep you from what will get you the most out of your career. The five chapters (most important and impactful first) will cover the following:

>> Clearly define your goals for college and force-rank.

>> Strictly and aggressively plan your college schedule. Cleverly revise it to get the most out of the fewest classes.

>> Break down the toughest projects into smaller chunks, setting deadlines well in advance and scheduling backwards.

>> Schedule each week into focused blocks—including fun.

» Hunt and eliminate waste in your schedule. Iterate.

Coupled with each chapter is a tool or app that's designed to make that step significantly easier, clearer, and more effective. Some of these are proprietary, and some I recommend getting elsewhere (I'll never try to create a new tool when there's another out there that'll get the job done well). Anything I recommend you get elsewhere is either free or (occasionally) costs a few bucks, and no, nobody's paying me to promote their stuff. For your added convenience, all tools and additional reading are available at: http://www.crush-college.com/tools.

In Part II, we're going to outline the **rules for daily effectiveness**, including how to take advantage of your environment, how to re-prioritize on the fly, and how to avoid breakdown when wrenches are thrown into the gears.

In Part III, we're going to build a process for sticking to your plan with **focus and motivation**. The tough part about being productive is not letting the new time you created decay into wasted time (more YouTube, etc). It's the result of years of book and article research, as well as testing with clients.

Beyond the principles and process, I have included tips and inspiration, including "the art of micro-efficiency" and "how to have 80% of your thesis done by the time you start." You'll learn how to read, write, design, and program (ha!) to maximize effectiveness… but as I said before, be wary of blindly following anyone else's personal style of work. These are my versions, which worked for me and those I worked with, but they may not be completely applicable to you.

That's it! Let's get to work. Don't put down this book until you've gotten through the Key Principles, written them down on a piece of paper, and stuck 'em to your bathroom mirror. And nope, I'm not even kidding.

Go Crush College, kid.

The Key Principles of Crushing College

There's a reason I use the somewhat ambiguous term "crush" when referring to how you'll engage your college experience.

There's a lot of information out there on how to get into grad school, land the great job, get published, et cetera. If you're looking for advice on what to do with your life, there's a lot of good reading out there—I provide a reading list in Part IV, "Closing," for those looking for more philosophical guidance. It's all very good, and I won't try to replicate it here.

With Crush College, however, we're going to liberate your time and direct it towards whatever of those life goals you believe are most important. The 12 Principles we're going to cover here will, if you embrace them and apply them, will lead you to stunning success with surprising ease. These principles are the basis of the step-by-step guide that follows in subsequent Parts, so pay attention: learn them, love them, internalize them.

First, just as in life, **you'll need to decide what you really want to get out of college** before you try to go after it more effectively. I'm going to guide you through that process, but I can't give you the perfect answer (or anything close to it). In my experience, those that loved college most had extremely varied paths. There are an overwhelming number of opportunities and options in college, and it would be lamentable to choose just a few to cover. Ultimately, though, the vast majority of options (clubs, majors, dorms, post-graduation tracks, etc) will have marginal impact on what's very important to you.

So we're going to have one over-arching goal throughout this entire process, which we will define as "crushing" (or "getting the most out of") college: **move as much time in your life as possible from what's less important to what's more important to you.** That's everything we'll be trying to do here.

To do this successfully, we must understand what possible goals or activities are more important than others. This is the hardest, but single most important part. Thus, our first principle:

1)   You must know in the depths of your heart and mind what is most important to you. These are your goals.

Not sure yet? That's good: the wise man will never truly be sure. Doubt is healthy. But to choose what you will and won't do with your time, your most powerful guide is your current belief of what's really important to you.

To elaborate a bit: if you want to be "productive," then you need to be working on what's most important to you. Cranking out papers, classes, resume-padders, or (god forbid) hours of work is pointless if it's not in touch with your deepest objectives.

> *An example: I abandoned efforts towards a "very publishable" thesis and a number of other papers. Why? I had a gut-check and went back to my goals in life… progressing into academia wasn't there at all. Besides stroking my ego, the effort of publishing my thesis would have done precious little for my career or my life and sucked up a whole lot of time. Once I realized that, it was an easy choice to make.*

The second principle, as some of you no doubt already see, follows directly from this:

2)   All of our goals must exist in a strict hierarchy.

Life is about making choices: all action is choosing one thing and foregoing another or others. Even among those things you've identified as most important to you, some will need to be greater than others in order for you to prioritize your choices.

In short, you won't be able to pursue all twenty of your most important goals with equal ferocity, so you must know what's #1 and what's #13 on the list to guide your planning, your dedication, and your action day-to-day—as hard as these choices are.

> *An example: In college I put graduating with the Master's degree in four years above continuing organized sports, even though I'd really loved them in high school. It was a very tough choice but by knowing which one was higher than the other, I was able to appropriately focus on one well and not do both poorly when the hammer hit the anvil later in my college career.*

Next, on the matter of making choices:

3)   Prioritization is about choosing what not to do.

Time is your most finite resource, and the most important decisions you make are about how you will use it—which means first deciding how not to use it. With a strong hierarchy of goals, we can reduce or eliminate those pursuits that are less important to us[1].

It's not always easy to cut down on or eliminate things we like—especially if they are habitual or give us short-term pleasure. But to get the most out of college, it's essential.

> *An example: In my last year, I had an "overloaded" my schedule with grad school classes, a thesis, and two jobs to support it (no student loans were available for Master's students). To handle all of this, I had to give up a lot. I quit the debate team, fraternity council, and all involvement in MIT politics. I reduced my gaming and partying to near-zero. It was, deep down, a whole lot more important for me to get my Master's, to not have to pay for another cripplingly expensive semester, and to (you may be seeing a theme here) get sleep.*

Besides that juggernaut of a semester, I was able to "have it all," but I had to make hard choices in the light of my real goals.

Now, in order to have it all you must embrace this:

---

1   If this sounds intimidating, consider this: video games, board games, cooking, sleeping, partying, and brewing beer are all high enough on my list of goals that they get their due time. Remember not to let anyone else veto what you believe your goals should be, no matter how highly you regard them.

4)   Far more improvement is possible than you believe.

Remember that MIT saying: "school, sleep, social: pick two." This statement alone, indoctrinated into the minds of impressionable freshmen arriving to campus, poisons them into believing there isn't a better way available to them. Because of the omnipresence of this "well-known truth," students feel they have no hope of improving when they find themselves drowning—everyone has already told them that the load is unreasonably great and they're just going to have to deal with it.

I rejected this notion on face. I believed that I could do more because I realized just how much time my colleagues and I were using ineffectively—in other words, there was a great amount of wasted time out there that I could redirect. As I systematically pursued that plan, I was shocked at just how much time I was able to salvage.

While this belief—this mindset—is not *sufficient*, it is absolutely necessary. (But if you're reading this book, there is a part of you that believes it already, isn't there?)

> *An example: The average college student spends over 1.5 hours/day on Facebook, and some good studies[2] see a strong correlation between this use and academic performance[3]. No surprise there. But a study of 2500 students[4] self-reported that they spend a whopping average of three hours per day texting[5]. Holy freakin' smokes! What could you do if you cut all that in half and had an extra 16 hours per week?*

There's a whole lot more out there, too. Almost anyone can identify that they spend too much time on Facebook, but what about too much time reading or in lab? Thus, we arrive at principle 5:

5)   View everything you do in terms of results only.

Could you spend too much time reading? Indeed! Consider: the number of pages (much less hours) you read is not a measure of success—reading is an *activity* rather than an *end* itself. *Why* do you read a particular book? For pleasure? To prepare for writing a paper? To learn a skill?

Measure your success in terms of how these ends are furthered. There is often opportunity to further these ends with less reading or a better method, such as increasing your reading speed through developing your skills.

---

2   http://www.academia.edu/1207833/Too_much_face_and_not_enough_books_The_relationship_between_multiple_indices_of_Facebook_use_and_academic_performance
3   There's a lot of variation on the actual number depending on the study—also no surprise.
4   http://blog.reyjunco.com/students-spend-a-lot-of-time-facebooking-searching-and-texting
5   Given that it's self-reported data, I personally suspect the real number is higher than three hours.

Reading is just a hypothetical example to get you thinking (though it may happen to be a big block of your time). Studying is similar (think "learning the key concepts," not "hours of studying").

> *An example: I reduced dramatically how much reading I did in my Master's year by thinking, before picking up each book, what the purpose of reading it was. Professors would assign large, dense books to read in a week, and I was doing this for four classes. Depending on what the purpose was (in-class discussion, preparation for a test, fodder for a paper, or something I was really interested in learning), I'd skim with a companion, read key chapters and skip others, supplement with short interpretation articles by other authors, or (if I absolutely had to) read the whole thing. (Given my own below-average reading speed, it would have been hopeless otherwise!)*

How, then, are we going to find all this time for the activities we've been told are *good*?

6)   In order to find truly significant amounts of time to redirect to your goals, you must aggressively challenge your assumptions and habits, and look deeply into *everything*.

When surveying how you spend your time, I want you to challenge every aspect of it. No activity is sacred, and no activity is *perfectly* geared towards your highest goals. Everything can be improved, always.

When you evaluate your time, look to exerting less effort in any given activity by learning how to do it smarter (there's plenty of material on the internet) or to do it more skillfully (increasing your reading speed and comprehension, for example).

> *An example: After college I was able to reduce the amount of time I slept from 7.5 hours to 6.3 by learning how to take a well-timed siesta that got me as much REM time as the regular 7.5 hours[6]. It was a dramatic revelation for me that even my precious, precious sleep time was not something in which "more time is always better."*

> *Another example, as I can't resist: In Chinese class I used to use flash-cards and simply wrote out characters over-and-over in rote memorization, as the Chinese did in the Confucian age. This consumed much time… and got me poor grades. But the Internet holds a vast trove of research on language learning: I found articles in free education journals, changed my methods dramatically, and reduced my time studying while improving my grades.*

In the book I'll suggest some places to find better methods for whatever goals you want to achieve, but the principle here is that *they are out there* and you're crazy not to go looking for them.

---

6   See The 4-Hour Body by Tim Ferriss. I can't always do this as life doesn't always let me have my siesta.

And since you're going to be experimenting with new methods:

7)   Measure *everything*.

How do we even know how much time we're spending on various activities? How do we know whether our efforts are making progress? Self-reporting by students (and all other humans) on these topics is notoriously inaccurate.

When you start hunting down wasted time, you'll need to measure how you spend all of your time, from the semester to the minute.

Why so vigilant? A few reasons:

> » Measuring will reveal all the time that you have to work with—without it, you're guessing and will underestimate how much you can improve and misjudge which activities to go after.

> » It's necessary to determine whether an implemented change or solution is working—if it's not, dump it.

> » By measuring *results* we can successfully find and embrace the methods that help us reach our goals faster or more effectively.

> » It will let you know if the recovered time is being used for your goals—or more Youtube!

> » By seeing measured success, we breed more motivation and propel ourselves further.

> *An example: After changing learning methods[7] for Chinese, my total study time was down more than 30% and my grades moved from a C average to Bs and As.*

Measuring my results was simple in this case—MIT provided the tests. For personal work, you may need to find tests yourself.

And when you do measure how you use your time, you may find a pattern emerging:

[7]   My only prayer in Chinese was highly prejudiced use of mnemonics for both sound and character, like this: http://remembereverything.org/keyword-method/

8)   80% of the results come in the first 20% of effort.

This is called "Pareto's Principle[8]" (or the 80/20 principle) after Vilfredo Pareto[9], a great Italian economist. It states that 80% of any effect comes from 20% of the sources[10]. So what does this mean for you?

» 80% of the results of any paper, skill, project, etc can be won with the right 20% of effort, which means there's huge opportunity to work more effectively.

» 80% of what you'll get out of college is on 20% of the activities you're probably doing.

» 80% of all recoverable time can be realized by changing only 20% of your habits.

This is great news: we don't have to change everything, only the few things that really matter. We don't have to do all the work in the sphere of our class, paper, project, et cetera.

Of course, this principle is approximate, and most of the time you will want to do better than 80% (unless you're happy being a B- student). But it makes clear that there are diminishing returns beyond that first 20% of effort (or 20% of activities), and that much of that diminishing effort not only can be *but should be* dropped entirely.

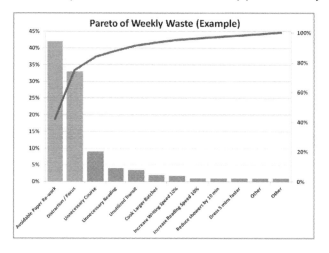

An example: While citing Wikipedia is a no-no, it's where I do almost all of my initial research. Turns out, Wikipedia is as accurate as Encyclopedia Brittanica[11]. For any

---

8   http://en.wikipedia.org/wiki/Pareto_principle
9   http://en.wikipedia.org/wiki/Vilfredo_Pareto
10   In his case he identified that 80% of wealth was owned by 20% of Italians. He also found that 20% of his pea plants in his garden produced 80% of the peas. He started seeing this everywhere. Luckily, it didn't end like the movie Pi: it caught on.
11   http://news.cnet.com/2100-1038_3-5997332.html

research paper, I gather my primary understanding of the topic, and even main points, from there. At this point, the research for the paper is often 80% done, and the other 20% is getting citations from institutionally accepted sources. This was far, far less effort than scouring those sources on their own, as Wikipedia (like any good encyclopedia) distills the key points of the information.

The 80/20 rule has further implications about where we should start looking to get time back:

9)   Save semesters and weeks before hours or minutes.

Saving ten hours per week is great. But if you want to stave off the risk of missing the four-year graduation mark (or if you want to get ambitious in adding classes, double majoring, or graduating early), you need to start by eliminating entire classes, projects, and commitments.

To do this, we must *first* look at the level of semesters and optimize our class load. Then we reduce weeks of work in major projects by doing the bulk of the work for those projects as regular class-work (rather than on top of it). Only *after* that does it make sense to evaluate how we spend our hours per week. It's the biggest stuff that will allow you to get super-human results.

> *An example: For my thesis, I chose a topic early and sequenced my classes in the three semesters before and the semester during writing it so that I was able to do the bulk of the research and writing as regular, graded work for those classes. I farmed these papers and notes when I started my thesis—I was already 80% done by the time I officially "started," without having done any extra work beyond what was required for the classes themselves. We'll go into this in more depth in Chapter Five, "Ruthlessly Eliminating Waste."*

> *Another example: I carefully studied the requirements and restrictions for majors and minors that seemed related. This allowed me to take a whopping six classes that counted towards two requirements (majors, minors, and basic graduation requirements), saving me essentially a semester and a half of work to get my degrees.*

The most effective way to recover semesters and weeks of time is by a simple method most college students ignore entirely:

10)   Invest in a great plan at all levels of work

Most college students don't plan out their classes through their careers at all—and certainly not as freshmen. Many bump around semester by semester and then by their senior year, forgotten requirements "sneak up" on them. I've seen people graduate late not because they failed classes, but because they failed to take one or two key required classes until it was too late.

Good planning is your best safeguard against going over four years and is step one of being able to add majors or graduate early. While a good plan is not sufficient in itself, it is absolutely necessary.

Investing up-front in a full plan, including classes, papers, clubs and activities, is a critical foundation for your college career.

An example: if I had planned more effectively, I could have actually graduated in 3.5 years with all the same degrees (or taken more classes that interested me) with only one additional five-class semester. Madness, but true.

Plans are great, but how do we to stick to them? The siren song of Facebook, Youtube, video games, and other forms of distraction is sometimes overwhelming. Thus:

11)   Take advantage of your human instincts instead of fighting them.

One dangerous instinct we have is to procrastinate, and usually we "fight" this by shaming ourselves, feeling guilty, or simply (and naively) telling ourselves we won't do it in the future. Nope! Doesn't work.

We are creatures of habit, with many forces pulling us in varied directions. We have a rational brain and a powerful evolved instinct, and we mistakenly think that the way to long-term success is to use the rational part of our brain to wrestle our instinct into submission.

But all sorts of great research on willpower[12] suggests that not only does this not work (in fact it often backfires and makes things worse), but it makes us miserable. Good news: by using the right psychological tricks, we can get our instincts to agree with our rational desires, or at least reduce the sweet calls to procrastination.

Here are a few of the ways to do this (we'll cover this in more detail later):

» Create clear "paintings" of your goals (like a picture of the former skinny you next to current heavier you)

» Write clear yes/no rules instead of ambiguous wants ("no sweets" rather than "eat less")

» Create objective, visual targets and tracking (like a graph of your total Facebook time against a target line)

---

12 A few good examples: Kelly McGonigal, The Willpower Instinct. Chip & Dan Heath, Switch. Johnathan Haidt, The Happiness Hypothesis.

> » Increase peer pressure (posting said Facebook time graph every week… on Facebook… for all your friends to see and heckle or congratulate, as is your due)

> » Put your money where your mouth is (one of my favorites: use the brilliant StickK[13] to put money in escrow and have them give it to one of your most-hated charities if you fail to meet your goal)

> » Lower barriers to good action (like sleeping in your gym clothes if you want to run in the morning)

> » Raise barriers to bad action (like using Firefox or Chrome extensions[14] that block websites during certain hours or after certain amounts of time on them)

> » Reduce the "bell and whistle" distractions (like turning off Facebook notifications and closing your email so you don't see new messages come in all the time)

> » Make a daunting task easier (by breaking it down into less-intimidating chunks, reducing the desire to procrastinate)

All of these affect your *instinctual* brain and either make it fight you less or make it your rational brain's ally. Consider these tools in your belt of how to keep yourself on target for a particular behavioral change you want to make. If you're having trouble breaking (or just starting to try breaking) old habits, start using your instincts to your advantage.

> *An example: For my weight-loss campaign last year, I posted an empty graph to Facebook with a target weight and a certain number of months to get there (Facebook is not totally useless!). I invited my friends to heckle me if I failed—I even got one to put up a $50 bet on me failing. I posted an updated graph every week to much fanfare (I was late one day and got completely hosed with jeering messages). Ultimately I got "only" 90% of the way to my target—I lost my $50, but dropped a whopping 31 lbs in three months. Knowing I was accountable to all these friends of mine made it a lot easier to put down the donut.*

But not all of the above are necessary, or are right for you. No one solution is going to change the game for you; everyone's different. And that's why:

12) Take on one major change at a time. Iterate like crazy. Re-evaluate everything you do. Drop what doesn't work.

You're going to adopt some new behaviors that don't make a major improvement. After measuring, if you don't see the improvement, either tweak the method (if there's a clear reason tweaking it will work) or dump it for a new one.

---

13   http://www.stickk.com/about.php
14   For Firefox I recommend Leechblock, and for Chrome I recommend StayFocusd. They're super.

For both the sake of not overwhelming your brain's capacity for change, and for the sake of effectively measuring what's working and what isn't, make few (maybe only one) major changes at a time. Don't try to boil the ocean—make progress, lock it in, celebrate, and move forward.

You'll learn new information about what you really want and what options are available to you as you go through college. It's critical to update your goals, your hierarchy, and your class plan as you go to make sure your time is directed at your top priorities. Do this at a routine frequency or after a revelation. This may even mean a change of majors[15]!

You'll estimate how much time a given task or activity will take, and will probably be wrong (especially after you make improvements). Update your project plans, weekly schedules, and daily routines as your estimates become more accurate.

Finally, you'll start to really believe in how much is possible when you start seeing early results. If you're interested in the "superhuman" college experience, you may find that you have more time for some lower priorities, and you may choose to take them on. After easily handling four classes, might you start taking five? Add gym time, add a new club, add a new personal project or hobby? It's up to you, but here is where you get to get aggressive, do more than you ever thought possible, and truly Crush College.

> *An example: I didn't decide to do a Master's degree until late in my college years. It was after making a number of changes in series (killing Reddit and Facebook, setting up better study habits, reducing reading, and effectively pre-planning major projects) that I saw the potential to take on more and harder classes and go after a Master's. After numerous successes, I had not only the free time but the confidence and momentum to shoot for the stars.*

---

15 Beware the passing whim! Think these revelations through and get advice on them before major life changes.

PART I
STEP-BY-STEP GUIDE TO RECLAIMING YOUR TIME

Now that we know the principles, we're going to start reclaiming your time, step by step. We'll be referring back to these principles briefly throughout Part 2, so go back and review if you need to.

Remember to implement these one step at a time, and certainly not faster than once per day.

Every step repeats at a set frequency. The more "high-level" the step, the longer the frequency. We start with the highest-level view both because it's the most important and because it drives more detailed steps.

Tools for each step are either included or are linked from the book. Completed examples of each step are always provided in the Cheat Sheets.

<u>A map of each chapter, by granularity of scope:</u>

The Career-Long Picture

Chapter 1: Creating Force-Ranked Goals

Chapter 2: Scheduling College for Success

The Semesterly Picture

Chapter 3: Crushing Each Semester

The Weekly Picture

Chapter 4: Crushing Each Week

The Hourly Picture

Chapter 5: Ruthlessly Eliminating Waste

A note on tools: for each Crush College tool referred to in the following chapters, detailed instructions are included wtihin the tool, so don't worry specifically about using them until you open them. For tools developed externally, a link is provided to a tutorial when possible.

I've also included a few screenshots to give you the idea, as well as a worked example at the end of each chapter.

The Career-Long Picture

At the career-long picture, we have two major steps: **creating force-ranked goals** and **scheduling college for success.**

CHAPTER 1 CREATING FORCE-RANKED GOALS

Frequency: *every year, or as revelations strike*

Total time: *a few hours (including conversations and meditations); varies*

Tools: *Crush College Goal-Setting Worksheet*
                (available at http://www.crush-college.com/tools)

As we've established, this is the single most important step in the whole process. Here we lay out your goals—that is, what you want to get out of college. Scary? It should be, at least a bit. That's why you've been putting it off. But we're going to do it *today*.

Keep in mind that it doesn't have to be perfect. Having a plan that feels "pretty good" is infinitely better than no plan. We're going to reiterate at least every year (and you can do so as frequently as your gut tells you to) and it will improve with each iteration. It may depart dramatically from where it was last time—this happened to me more than once. Get advice and input from your friends and family where it makes sense[1], but don't let anyone bully you into going after *their* goals over yours.

These goals will guide all of our planning into the future. Remember the key principle: if your work isn't supporting or furthering these goals, it's wasted. If we can get more results in terms of these goals by changing our methods, it's an opportunity to recover more time.

---

1   I can't stress how helpful this is. Professors, older friends, peers, and family provide huge insight and
     perspective that you will inevitably lack from only having the opportunity to live life as yourself.

For further inspiration and guidance on this, I suggest Cal Newport's <u>How to Win at College</u>.

To make it simpler, we're going to break down the goal-setting process into four parts:

A. **Setting Clear High-Level Goals.** This is an abstract exercise designed to put you in touch with what you really want to get out of college

B. **Breaking Down Goals into Smaller Actions.** This drives clarity and forces goals into a state where you can act on them (that is, they are "actionable")

C. **Force-Ranking Your Goals.** This tells you what's ultimately most important among many goals and is necessary to decide how to spend your limited time

D. **Associating Activities with Your Goals.** These activities will be what we actually schedule in our plans

A.   Setting Clear High-Level Goals

What we're going to do first is paint a broad picture. I'm going to provide very little structure for this, as I've found doing so only frustrates the process. It's time for you to get creative.

I want you to express, as well as you can, in sentences, or in pictures, or in interpretive dance, what you want out of college. Ideally, what will it look like? What will you do? What comes next? What will you feel? What will you look back on in 60 years and smile upon with a deep, inner satisfaction? This is it. My only guidance is the following semi-comprehensive categorization of goals (in no specific order of importance):

» Health

» Preparation for what's after college (grad school, industry, entrepreneurship, etc)

» Development of other life skills and habits

» Personal intellectual fulfillment and exploration

» Social fulfillment

» Creative or spiritual fulfillment

» Family contact

» Financial stability

» Relaxation and fun

Enjoy this exercise. Get help from friends, think about it, bounce things around. A few tips:

a. Look to whatever your school offers in majors, clubs, sports, extracurricular activities, study-abroad, living groups, and all sorts of other stuff. Use this as inspiration.

b. Write down ideas even if you're not sure you really care about them. We'll force-rank them later.

c. Don't sell short your desire for relaxation, but be deliberate and explicit about what you want in it, rather than vague. Even "watch a movie" or "take a nap" is great—if you know you like them and explicitly go enjoy them, you're getting something out of it[2].

B. Breaking Down Goals into Smaller Actions

All right, nice work. Our next step is to break down these high-level goals into discrete actions that can be assembled into a plan. At the end of this section, each of your goals should be shaping up into a set of actions that you're going to choose to do more of or less of. Your goals should be:

» **Actionable:** They need to be things you can do.

» **Comprehensive:** They need to encapsulate all categories of your life, including and beyond academics, including things as simple as sleeping a certain amount, helping friends with academics or other needs, dating, cooking so often per week (if that's your thing), et cetera—you want to make sure you are thinking about the whole picture.

» **Specific:** They should refer to a very clear part of your life—"be healthy" is junk. If you want to lose weight, increase your cardiovascular endurance, or sleep more, *then* we're getting somewhere.

» **Measurable and Targeted:** There should be a way to measure whether the goal is "complete" or not. Not everything can be measured in numbers, but where it can, make sure you do it. "Lose weight" is insufficient—"Lose 5% body fat" is much better. A yes/no measurement is fine, too ("don't do narcotics").

» **Bounded:** Your goals must be limited, or have a deadline: "graduate within 4 years," rather than simply "graduate," et cetera.

2   One of the reasons I'm so passionate about this point is we "recharge" or otherwise feel the power of relaxing when we go do something deliberate in order to relax. We *don't* if we're undirected, like just wasting time on the Internet.

Why is this so important? I want you to be able to look back on these in a year or two and either say confidently, "yes, I am on track to meet that goal" or, "no, I'm not." I also want to make sure you are able to effectively turn these into the actions or activities that will make them happen.

<u>Step by step:</u>

1. **Take each high-level goal and break it down into multiple goals (if necessary).** A good example may be having many criteria for good health or strong preparation for post-college, all of which you want met. Separate all those criteria into different parts. List these in the "Detailed Goals" page of the Crush College Goal-Setting Worksheet.

2. **Define success for each detailed goal.** If you can clearly say, "here's how I'll look back and know it went well," then you're either one step away from a goal with a *target*, or you're as close as you're ever going to be.

3. **Fill your goals with the other necessary details above.** Does it have a due date? Is the goal something actionable?

4. **Break down goals even further, where appropriate.** "Get into grad school" is a great goal, but not detailed enough to be able to schedule work into a plan. What implications does this have for your grades, your thesis, what track you take in your major, what recommendations you get?

A quick example:

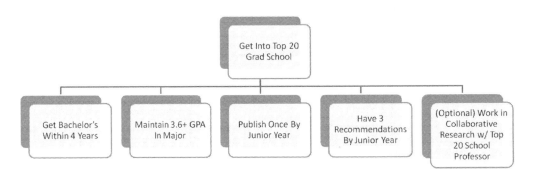

At this point you'll have a list of pretty clear goals that look somewhat similar in syntax and form.

A parting note on iterating this process: your first iteration is going to suck. Seriously. You'll leave out critical goals that you haven't thought of. In the next week, you may get a friend requesting help. "But helping friends isn't on my goal list!" you say. Well, realistically, it probably should be. These kinds of unexpected priorities will pop up all the time, and you'll need to be vigilant about updating your goals to reflect that. If you don't, your goal sheet will become increasingly irrelevant to the point that you no longer use it, and you'll be right back where you started. No good! In short: inspiration to iterate will strike frequently within the first few weeks of making your list—make sure you follow through.

C.   Force-Ranking Your Goals

All right, great. That was hard. You've slept on it, and now for something even harder: force-ranking. This means that you list your goals in order of priority, from one to however many goals you have. No ties allowed.

"Why?" You ask. "They're all important." It's true, they are. But there will come a time (many, many times) when you need to choose to pursue some of these more than others. Knowing which are the most important is key. The goals further down the list don't have to get *no attention*, but they're going to get less attention than the goals higher on the list. Surprisingly, you may still spend more time per week on a lower-down goal (like sleeping, unless it's numero uno) than a higher-up one. So this force-ranking is about how much focus, attention, and care we put into something—not necessarily about time. It's a way for us to make choices between multiple goals when the going gets tough.

Step by step:

1. **Open your Goal-Setting Worksheet.** You'll have your goals listed there with space to place numbers in the columns to the right.

2. **Select a number for each one!** Try out different rankings and see how they feel (as you put down numbers, they'll auto-sort into your force-ranked list). It should have some emotional resonance for you. Ask yourself for any two adjacent goals, "if I had to choose between these two, would I choose the one above?" If so, you're doing great. If not, adjust your ranks.

    Here you can also get creative about setting *graduated* goals. For example, I may have a goal of "Get a 3.7+ GPA" and another graduated goal of "Get a 3.5+ GPA." The second might be more important than getting 7 hours of sleep per night, but the former may not be. So in our ranking, we may have:

    1) *Average at least five hours of sleep per night*

    2) *3.5+ GPA*

    3) *Average at least seven hours of sleep per night*

4) *3.7+ GPA*

5) *Get a healthy breakfast of Cocoa Sugar Bombs ever day*

6) *...et cetera*

Like in Step 1, you may need to reiterate this fairly often in the first few weeks as you realize that you're not willing to be late to a test just to eat your Cocoa Sugar Bombs in the morning.

Below is a very brief example from the Crush College Goal-Setting Worksheet:

Health	CR	Post-College Prep	CR
Sleep at least 6 hours/night	2	Get bachelor's within 4 years	1
Sleep at least 7 hours/night	5	Maintain 3.6+ GPA	3
Lose 5% of body fat	7	Publish Once by Junior year	6
Run 10k/week	8	Have 3 Recommendations by Junior Year	4
		Work in Collaboration w/ Top 20 Professor	10

D.   Associating Actions with These Goals

With force-ranked goals, we need to briefly make sure we have clear actions associated with each of them. Some of these will be laughably simple (what's the action for "get 7.5 hours of sleep?"). Other goals will yield fruit through this exercise.

A quick example: lose 5% body fat" should have associated actions, like a certain kind exercise, a workout frequency, a particular diet, and a frequency of measurement (ah, the part people most often forget!).

All of the associated actions for these goals should be:

» Something one could hypothetically put in a calendar

» Easy to describe in terms of location, environment, tools, et cetera

» Matched, as appropriate, to offerings from your school

Don't worry here about listing out (for example) every single class associated with graduating—it's an unnecessary bureaucratic burden, and I suspect you know how I feel about those. Do your research as necessary and add actions that will bring clarity and direction when we're building plans and when we're making decisions in real-time.

The Final Word: Be in Touch With your Heart

Most students bounce around college with little direction. *It's not psychologically easy to commit to a direction*. But I guarantee it is better to go down the *wrong* direction than to have none at all. You don't need to commit to these goals for life, but if you fail to commit to any, you won't accomplish any.

Furthermore, the best way to gain clarity on whether a goal resonates with your heart is by running towards it. Don't be afraid to change once you know in your deepest self that a goal is wrong for you. Beware the whim, but beware also non-commitment based in fear. Fear is the mind-killer.

Remember: Review Yearly!

Review this *at least* every year and reiterate. Are your goals the same? What's changed? What's on track and what's in trouble? Let this guide you in altering plans for the next semesters.

Example 1: Sample Force-Ranked Goals

These aren't exactly what my scribbled notes of goals looked like eight years ago, but they're close (and a bit easier to read). This isn't a comprehensive list—my purpose is to make a point rather than overwhelm you with text.

Force-Ranked Goals	Associated Activities
Bachelors degree within 4 years	Standard set of classes; set & review plan
Average 6+ hours sleep/night	--
3.5+ GPA	Schedule office hrs for any classes at B- or lower; cut goof-off time if GPA drops
Spend fulfilling quality time with 6 closest friends	Schedule lunches & dinners at least 1/mo with each. Allow spontaneous distraction with them 2-3 times/work week
Employed "gainfully" within 6 months of graduating	Strong resume through internships each summer & research once/ school year
Degree in a field I absolutely love	Explore 4-5 majors and pick one
Help my friends in their hours of greatest need	Allow spontaneous distraction as necessary. Have early conversations that clarify intent/boundaries
Get "out" at least once/week	Schedule in--Fridays or Saturdays, usually
Masters degree within 4 years	Squeeze schedule; allow 5 classes/semester up to once/year; start thesis early; get permission sophomore year
Average 7+ hours sleep/night	--
Blog on Foreign Policy at least 1x/week	Schedule in time; keep running list of ideas
3.7+ GPA	Over-schedule classes with B's; tutoring for anything below B-
At least 1 gaming night / month	Get in schedule
Masters degree within 4.5 years	Basic class schedule + start thesis early
Keep debt below $100k	Pick up paid summer jobs & paid term research (this double-dips into resume)

With clear goals in place, we're going to next make our first major plan to achieve them. Starting at the highest level, we're going to plan our college careers, end-to-end.

CHAPTER 2 SCHEDULING COLLEGE FOR SUCCESS

Frequency: *every semester, or as revelations strike*

Total time: *up to six hours the first time; about one hour thereafter*

Tools: *Crush College Career Planner (available at http://www.crush-college.com/
                  tools), your university's website*

Starting as early as possible (hopefully before you register for your first classes!), have a great plan. This is the **single most important component** to graduating on time. It was also a big part in how I graduated in four years with a major, two minors, and a Master's degree, despite switching majors twice.

I've found that almost no freshmen and very few upperclassmen have this kind of a plan. The desire to "find oneself" has us fly by the seat of our pants. Most university require-ments have enough "buffer" built in that you can misstep and graduate on time… but (I can't harp on this enough) 60% of students *don't* graduate on time, and it's not because they're failing. They. Lack. A. Plan. If you effectively build a plan, even if you stop reading this book there, you won't end up a statistic.

There are four basic sections to building an effective plan, the latter three of which are designed to challenge and improve said plan.

A. **Build a Four-Year Schedule**

B. **Re-build for Efficiency**

C. **Challenge the Schedule by Reducing a Semester**

D. **Optional: Iterate for Added Flexibility**

By the end we'll have a beautiful plan that even your academic advisor will admire.

A. Just Build a Darn Plan Already: Step by Step

You'll want to have the Crush College Career Planner handy as you follow the below steps.

1. **Pick your major** (and minors, etc). You might not know what it's going to be. If not, that's fine—pick a plausible one anyway (and keep a list of other plausible majors). If you're having trouble deciding, take some time in Section D for a concentrated "exploration" to help you make a decision on a reasonable schedule.

2. **List all requirements.** This includes general graduation requirements, major requirements, and minor requirements[1].

3. **Compile a list of all classes**, including when they run.

4. **Pick key electives** for your major, grad requirements, etc. Aren't sure? Pick something plausible. These tend to come later so they're easiest to change as you learn more.

   a) This will likely include a sub-field for your major, and a thesis or final project if relevant. If your major doesn't have defined specializations or sub-fields, make sure you determine to create your own coherent concentration of some sort.

   b) Pick graduation requirement electives that deeply interest you, help you advance your goals, contribute to a minor or second major (if interested), et cetera. (More on double-dipping later.)

   c) Feel welcome to keep a few options of majors or concentrations available to you in your later years. Just put multiple classes into a single slot in the Career Planner or keep multiple copies of the Career Planner for each major/concentration that you're considering.

5. **Build a prerequisite chain.** Start with the *end* electives in mind and then back-fill prerequisites until you've reached classes with none. Your school website should

---

1   If you've taken classes or have AP, IB, or transfer credits, list those as well and match them to requirements. Tick those requirements off the list.

tell you what prerequisites are required for each class, so you should be able to link further "upstream" until you find the base classes.

6. **Match the electives and prerequisite chain to your requirements.** This will make sure you're covering all the bases for your major and graduation requirements, taking neither too many (wasteful) nor too few (not meeting all requirements) classes. Write these in a classes list.

7. **Identify schedule gaps.**

   a) First, go back to your requirements list and add classes to your classes list that fulfill anything that wasn't crossed off. At this point you should have all basic requirements met.

   b) Odds are good at this point that you don't have four classes per semester for the above. You may be *short on credits*. Great—identify these as a spot for a second major, minor, study abroad, etc.

8. **Populate a schedule, *backwards*.** Start with four classes per semester, with your final project and final electives. From there, populate backwards using your pre-requisite chain. Other classes that don't exist in any "chains" should be added to put the appropriate work burden on each semester and make sure you're not bored to tears at any point.

9. **Add non-class goals.** Going straight down your priority list, incorporate your goals that aren't related to class-work, in order. This includes sleep, sports, clubs, your own reading, social time—whatever is on your list. If you haven't yet, find the specifics of activities or offerings at your school that correspond to your goals[2]. All in all, we need to answer the question of "how much can we take on in a semester?" You'll have to use your gut to a large extent, but here's a rough way to be more scientific about recurring commitments (rather than, say, a study-abroad):

   a) You have 168 hours in a week.

   b) Let's assume 10% of it is "slop" time—that is, lost in transition and confusion—for now. It's probably lower than that, but we can get more aggressive later. That gives us 151 hours.

   c) Subtract total time for classes (at most schools, a 3-credit class expects 12 hours of work per week, on average). That said, as you'll see below, you can do a lot better. My "peak" productivity was about 6 hours/week per class; I will estimate 8 in my example below.

---

2   If you want to swing dance, find the swing dance club. Etc.

d) Subtract sleep, morning and evening transition to and from bed, meals, transit, shopping for food, laundry, and anything else necessary for living comfortably. Estimate for now; later we'll compile data (through time studies, which we'll cover in Chapter Five, "Ruthlessly Eliminating Waste").

e) The time you have left after all of this is what you have available for any other pursuit. Make some estimate of total weekly time for a pursuit; some have very high variability (like "pleasure reading" or "socializing"). For now, you'll have to pick something that works and modify as time goes on. If you have *too much* leftover time, add more goals into the list.

In the Crush College Career Planner, you can add the weekly recurring goals that you're going to pursue to the "Weekly Pursuits" page, and it will do the math for you. Keep this around, as we'll be using it later to plan each week!

Here's an example:

Priority	Hours per Week
Classes (4)	32
Sleep	52.5
Transit	7
Morning Routine	3.5
Evening Routine	3.5
Laundry	1
Meals (cook + eat)	7
Food Shopping	2
Socializing	12
Undergrad Senate	4
Pleasure Reading	7
Gaming	4
Gym	6
Other Goofing Off	6
Social Media	3.5
Total Remaining	**0**
Originally Available	**151**

So here we really start to put our force-ranking of priorities to the test. Which ones aren't on there at all? Does that seem right? Otherwise, what should change? Remember that it's a rough approximation, but gives you a decent idea of where you "cut off" the list between what you're really going to pursue and what not. It will also help you see what lower-priority items are available to be reduced or eliminated when unexpected additional work inevitably comes up. Like everything else, there's no perfect answer here, so you'll need to be rigorous about re-evaluating this as time goes on.

You may end up making huge changes to the method described in this chapter to keep more options open. You might create a number of plans for different majors, and then synthesize them to make the first few semesters equally optimal for all paths. Don't be constrained, but the bottom line is: just make the plan(s).

Example 1: MIT's General and Mechanical Engineering Degree Requirements

Doing the math here shows us we can get our MechE degree with 28 classes, giving us 4 free classes even if we only want to take 4 classes per semester. We can either add valuable classes or take some pressure off during the toughest semesters.

Bachelor of Science in Mechanical Engineering/Course 2

General Institute Requirements (GIRs)	Subjects
Science Requirement	6
Humanities, Arts, and Social Sciences Requirement	8
Restricted Electives in Science and Technology (REST) Requirement [can be satisfied by 2.001 and 18.03 in the Departmental Program]	2
Laboratory Requirement [can be satisfied by 2.671 in the Departmental Program]	1
Total GIR Subjects Required for SB Degree	17

Communication Requirement

The program includes a Communication Requirement of 4 subjects:

2 subjects designated as Communication Intensive in Humanities, Arts, and Social Sciences (CI-H); and 2 subjects designated as Communication Intensive in the Major (CI-M) [satisfied by 2.009 and 2.671 in the Departmental Program].

PLUS Departmental Program	Units

Subject names below are followed by credit units, and by prerequisites, if any (corequisites in italics).

Required Departmental Core Subjects	159

2.001 Mechanics and Materials I, 12, REST; Physics I (GIR), Calculus II (GIR), *18.03*

2.002 Mechanics and Materials II, 12; 2.001*, Chemistry (GIR)

2.003J Dynamics and Control I, 12, REST; Physics I (GIR), 18.03

2.004 Dynamics and Control II, 12; 2.003J*, Physics II (GIR)

2.005 Thermal-Fluids Engineering I, 12, REST; Physics II (GIR), Calculus II (GIR), *18.03*

2.006 Thermal-Fluids Engineering II, 12; 2.005*, 18.03*

2.008 Design and Manufacturing II, 12, 1/2 LAB; 2.007*

2.009 The Product Engineering Process, 12, CI-M; 2.001*, 2.003J*, 2.005*, 2.008*; senior standing or permission of instructor

Prerequisites are listed after the course name and hours.

2.086 Numerical Computation for Mechanical Engineers, 12; Physics I (GIR), Calculus II (GIR), 18.03

2.670 Mechanical Engineering Tools, 3[1]

2.671 Measurement and Instrumentation, 12, LAB, CI-M; 2.001*, 2.003J*, Physics II (GIR)

18.03 Differential Equations, 12, REST; Calculus II (GIR)

2.ThU Undergraduate Thesis, 6[2]
and
2.007 Design and Manufacturing I, 12; 2.001*
or
2.017J Design of Electromechanical Robotic Systems, 12, 1/2 LAB; 2.003J*, 2.005*, 2.671

2.672 Project Laboratory, 6, 1/2 LAB; 2.001, 2.003J, 2.006, 2.671
or
2.674 Micro/Nano Engineering Laboratory, 6; 2.001*, 2.003J*, 2.005*, 2.671*

Restricted Electives   24

Students are required to take two of the following elective subjects (substitutions by petition to the MechE Undergraduate Office):

2.016 Hydrodynamics, 12; Physics II (GIR), 18.03

2.017J Design of Electromechanical Robotic Systems, 12, 1/2 LAB; 2.003J*, 2.005*, 2.671

2.019 Design of Ocean Systems, 12, CI-M; 2.001, 2.003J, 2.005*; senior standing or permission of instructor

2.050J Nonlinear Dynamics I: Chaos, 12; 18.03*, Physics II (GIR)

2.092 Computer Methods in Dynamics, 12; 2.001*, 2.003J*

2.12 Introduction to Robotics, 12; 2.004*

2.14 Analysis and Design of Feedback Control Systems, 12; 2.004*

2.184 Biomechanics and Neural Control of Movement, 12; 2.004*

2.370 Molecular Mechanics, 12; 2.001*; Chemistry (GIR)

2.51 Intermediate Heat and Mass Transfer, 12; 2.006*

2.60J Fundamentals of Advanced Energy Conversion, 12; 2.006*

2.184 Biomechanics and Neural Control of Movement, 12; 2.004*

2.370 Molecular Mechanics, 12; 2.001*; Chemistry (GIR)

2.51 Intermediate Heat and Mass Transfer, 12; 2.006*

2.60J Fundamentals of Advanced Energy Conversion, 12; 2.006*

2.71 Optics, 12; Physics II (GIR), 18.03; 2.004*

2.72 Elements of Mechanical Design, 12; 2.005*, 2.007, 2.671

2.793J Fields, Forces and Flows in Biological Systems, 12; 2.005*

2.797J Molecular, Cellular, and Tissue Biomechanics, 12; 2.370, 18.03*

2.813 Environmentally Benign Design and Manufacturing, 12; 2.008*

2.96 Management in Engineering, 12

Departmental Program Units That Also Satisfy the GIRs   (36)

Unrestricted Electives[3]   48

Total Units Beyond the GIRs Required for SB Degree   195

A thesis! I bet you can do most of this in a few well-planned classes.

This means "two of them."

See "with permission of instructor?" That's gold.

This, plus general requirements, can be done in seven semesters with four classes each semester.

Building your plan is the most important part… but it's just the beginning.

B.   Re-build the Schedule for Efficiency: Step by Step

This is where we get clever. The principles for this step are to **take advantage of classes that fill multiple requirements** (e.g.: grad requirements plus minor or second major, et cetera) and **take classes that will do some of the work for your thesis/final project** if you have one. In other words, you're going to create a schedule that lets you *do more with the same number of classes*. Maybe you don't want to. Do this exercise anyway—you're going to see how easy college can be and how aggressive you can get. The thing to keep in mind here is that you may very well want to take classes that don't contribute to a degree because they really interest you. This is fine—just keep in mind where everything fits in your goal hierarchy.

1.   **Find classes that only fulfill graduation requirements**. All of these are "inefficient" if they aren't either fulfilling a personal goal or adding "meat" to your degree. Particularly inefficient classes are those you're taking *only* to get enough credits to graduate.

2.   **Rigorously hunt down alternatives and replace them**. For example: if you're an engineer and have Humanities/Social Sciences graduation requirements, get a minor in a language. Similarly, make sure all possible graduation requirements are fulfilling prerequisites for your major, and vice versa.

3.   **Test out of classes**. If you're a freshman (or in some schools, even if you're not), you can almost certainly test out of a number of classes. Most schools (even MIT) have little confidence that you have the education to skip their basic writing, science, or math requirements, and make you take classes you have aced before unless you pass these tests. Show 'em you know your stuff.

4.   **Do *not* front-load basic (non-major) graduation requirements**. The earlier you take foundation classes for your major (or possible majors), the earlier you can branch out to advanced classes in your major and the earlier you can lock down what your major is and finalize your schedule. Don't take "writing" in your first semester if you're considering three different engineering degrees.

5.   **Match classes, co-ops, research, et cetera to publications, thesis, et cetera**. Want to get published? Great—get paid to do it with research or a co-op, or take a class with a final paper in a topic you might want to publish. Challenge yourself here and get ambitious!

6.   **Optional: pick two majors with many shared requirements**. Math and Computer Science, Art and History, International Relations and Language. You'll broaden

horizons and beef your resume. There are a shocking number of classes that either *do* or *can* double count (see "ask for more") between two majors and you should absolutely go get them[3]. I know a number of folks at MIT that opted for the Computer Science and Math double major because the number of overlapping classes made it comparatively easy.

7. **Ask for more.** Asking is hugely powerful. I got unorthodox permission to get some of the grad-level classes in my major to *double-count* for my Master's and my Bachelor's requirements. It was awesome. Ask to have the rules bent or boundaries pushed for you. Often admins have the ability to sign a piece of paper and make wild exceptions if you're able to justify why they're a good idea. Nobody will get angry at you for asking, I promise[4].

Example 2: MIT and the Easiest Minors (or Second Majors) Ever

Employers and grad schools start drooling when they see folks come out with multiple majors. Since you have to take classes outside your major, you might as well get the credit for it on your degree. Let's look at an example of how to do this at MIT.

Let's say you're an engineer or scientist, because it's MIT, and you're 90% likely to be one. To graduate, you need to take eight classes in Humanities, Arts, and Social Sciences (HASS):

General Institute Requirements (GIRs)	Subjects
Science Requirement	6
Humanities, Arts, and Social Sciences Requirement	8
Restricted Electives in Science and Technology (REST) Requirement [can be satisfied by 2.001 and 18.03 in the Departmental Program]	2
Laboratory Requirement [can be satisfied by 2.671 in the Departmental Program]	1
Total GIR Subjects Required for SB Degree	17

Most MIT students gripe their butts off about this and then just take the classes that have reputations for being easy (or at least don't have class at 9am). What a tragic waste! A whole two semesters' worth of work, up in a puff of smoke!

If you look close enough at these HASS requirements (many don't and get a nasty surprise in senior year!), you need a "concentration" of three classes in the same area that needs to be approved by a HASS professor. Three other classes need to be in fields outside of this "concentration."

Now, since we need a concentration anyway, why not go for a minor? Two minutes of research reveals that **almost every HASS minor at MIT is six classes, five of which can**

3   A second major means career flexibility and often means a higher starting salary by default.
4   I heard "no" very, very often and "yes" a few key times. I was a topic of humor for some admins, but they love being able to help students—that's why they're there—and will do what they can.

count towards your general graduation requirements! Voila—you show up to MIT one class away from a minor. *Almost nobody does this*. It's bonkers. Remember: to graduate with a coveted Mechanical Engineering degree, you have *four extra classes* hanging around!

Looking at East Asian studies, we see that we can take three classes outside of MIT to count for this. Summer abroad, anyone? Fill out a sufficiently rad application and MIT will cover the travel and housing. Your school might just do the same—you've just got to look and ask.

Minor in Asian and Asian Diaspora Studies

The Minor Program in Asian and Asian Diaspora Studies is designed for students interested in the language, history, politics, and culture of Asia. The geographic region of Asia includes countries such as Bangladesh, China, India, Japan, Korea, Mongolia, Pakistan, the Philippines, Taiwan, and Vietnam. In consultation with the minor advisor, students may focus their coursework on a sub-region of Asia, on one of the Asian diasporas, or design their program to offer a comparative study across different regions and/or cultural groups.

The goal of the Minor Program is to provide balanced coverage of language, humanistic, and social science offerings and to expose students to comparative perspectives.

The Minor Program in Asian and Asian Diaspora Studies consists of six subjects (at least three of which must be MIT subjects) arranged in four areas of study:

Area I: Language
Area II: Humanities and the Arts
Area III: Social Sciences
Area IV: Historical Studies

The language requirement can be satisfied by taking two intermediate (Levels III and IV) subjects in an Asian language. Students with proficiency at this level in the spoken and written language can either take two more advanced language subjects (highly recommended), or two more courses from Areas II, III and IV. Chinese and Japanese are taught at MIT. Other languages may be taken at Harvard, Wellesley, or during the summer with permission from relevant transfer credit examiner.

This screams "Summer in China."

As with all HASS Minors, only five of the six minor subjects may be counted toward the 8-subject Institute HASS Requirement. Of these five, at most one (1) shall count toward satisfaction of the HASS Distribution Requirement.

You already need to take 5 of 6 classes here.

A HASS second major works the same way. If you only get a HASS major, you can't double-dip your HASS graduation requirement and your major. But if it's a second major, you can do just that (this is a little-known technicality—do your research!). For example, you can get a History or Philosophy major by taking five classes beyond those necessary to graduate with your first degree, if it is your second major. Since you already have four free class spaces (for the example MechE degree), how could you say no? That's two majors with only one semester of five classes.

For those who were HASS majors, the Science, "REST," and Lab requirements similarly dovetail *quite beautifully* into an engineering or science minor while only taking one or two extra classes. Science and Engineering minors or second degrees do wonders for your paycheck.

The bottom line is that there are pretty magical things you can do out there by double-dipping—that is, taking classes that fulfill multiple requirements simultaneously. Most people don't do it not because it's hard, but because they just don't look—and that's just a shame.

C.   Challenge the Schedule and Reduce a Semester: Step by Step

We get daring here. We're going to move four classes and plan cleverly to do the whole thing in seven semesters. This means a few semesters with five classes, unless you've tested out of or otherwise taken care of a good number. It might not interest you now, but just like with Section B, you might decide to get aggressive later once you see how easy your academics can be.

1. **Identify your four easiest semesters.** You'll inevitably have easier semesters and harder ones, depending on your classes. Find the four easiest—they're out there. If you have a pass/fail semester, that counts. MIT has a pass/no-record system for the first term to help people adjust (no grades on your report card—you either pass, or the class doesn't show up on your transcript at all. You're envious, I know).

2. **Identify the four easiest classes in the other four semesters.** You probably see where this is going…

3. **Distribute the four easy classes to the four easy semesters**. These five-class semesters will probably be approximately as hard as your four harder four-class semesters.

4. **Re-configure your schedule to be seven semesters long.** Don't want to graduate early? That's fine—you can take four more classes this way. This might be enough

for a second major if you're taking advantage of multiple-requirement classes. Build yourself a buffer in case things go wrong—that way, the "oh shit" semester is your eighth, not your ninth. **I know this is scary**. But remember we're going to make you hugely effective week-to-week. You'll be able to handle five classes more easily than your colleagues can handle four.

D. Optional - Iterate for Added Flexibility: Step by Step

If you don't know what you want your major to be, build your schedule to make sure you figure it out as quickly as possible, rather than wasting your time switching later (as I did!). If you're considering multiple majors, great! As you have seen above, you have room for extra classes. I highly encourage freshman fall or spring being the "exploration" semester in which you take some of the "typical" classes (not the least or most enjoyable of the bunch) of a few majors—maybe three or four—to get a feel for each major and hopefully either pick one or severely narrow the field.

1. **Pick the majors you want to explore.**

2. **Pick the foundational class for each major that is most telling of what the major's like**. Every major has fun and awful classes—don't go for either. Get a sense of the *topic*—"do I want to do this when I graduate?" If these fulfill other graduation requirements, *even better*.

3. **Schedule them for your first semester or two**. First semester, if possible. If you scheduled well above, *you have spots in your schedule you need to fill to get enough credits*. This means no five-class semesters necessary to do your exploring. Most of your classmates will be taking core graduation requirement classes. You can take them later. Do *not* delay figuring out what you want your major to be.

   If you're a crazy bastard… you can overload this semester with six or seven classes and plan to drop the least exciting ones before your school's drop date to get more exploration for your buck. The risks here are first that your academic advisor might cough up a hairball at the idea, and second that you'll be tempted to continue on with all of them for the sake of it. Even if it doesn't beat you into the dust, just remember: wasted time isn't just less Facebook, it's taking classes that don't really add to your personal goals.

4. **Plan for a minor or second major**. These foundational classes should prompt you to pick a major. If you're still stuck between two, plan for one of them to convert to a minor or second major. That way, when you decide, your exploratory time won't have been wasted, but will have been a major contribution to the overall degree(s).

The Final Word: Plan Deliberately

In my experience, there were two camps at MIT: those that planned every class, project, co-op, research, internship, etc, very deliberately… and those that didn't. The former group *universally* had beefier degrees, faster completion times, better jobs, and less stress. The latter often struggled. **Don't skip this.**

Check in on this plan and re-iterate every single semester, whether you think you're on track or not.

Example 3: Erik's Actual College Schedule

Note that while my schedule is pretty awesome, it could have been better. I didn't plan well from the beginning. **Yours can be even better than mine below.** Also note I only had two semesters where I needed to take five classes.

Things to Note Overall:

» I worked on my thesis for *four semesters*, using other requirement classes five times.

» Some of my classes contributed to two minors, or minor and major, or major and Master's.

» I should have tested out of Physics 1, Calculus 1, and Biology 1—I sadly simply failed to bother.

» MIT has a "January Term" where one has many options. I took two classes total. See below.

» MIT has a "Humanities/Arts/Social Sciences" concentration requirement. I use "HASS" below to denote this.

» Anything in the schedule in "sneer quotes" means I intended that benefit, but later changed my mind.

» The job I planned for was in the CIA or State Department. I switched to consulting last-minute.

What I got out of it (well, all that is quantifiable):

» Bachelors: **Political Science** (13 classes, including four overlaps with Master's, thesis)

» Masters: **Political Science—International Relations** (six Master's classes, research, thesis)

» Minor: **Mechanical Engineering** (Five MechE classes plus Differential Equations)

» Minor: **International Studies** (Five classes plus research on China—had to ask for rule tweak here)

» Humanities Concentration: Chinese (Chinese IV plus three humanities classes on China)

» **Two published papers** (I got lazy and didn't publish my thesis after switching majors)

» **Three stellar recommendations** (and I could have gotten more)

Erik's Actual College Schedule

Classes & Benefits	Freshman Semester 1	Freshman Semester 2	Freshman Summer 1	Sophomore Semester 3	Sophomore Semester 4	Sophomore Summer 2	Junior Semester 5	Junior Semester 6	Junior Summer 3	Senior Semester 7	Senior Semester 8
Class 1	Comp Design	Diff Equations	Compsci Intern	MechE Statics 1	MechE Ctrls 2	Research Job 1	Intro Biology	E Asia Int'l Rel'n	Consult Intern	Thesis Proposal	Thesis
Benefits	Compsci "major"	Eng'ring "major," minor	$$, Compsci exploration	MechE "major," minor	MechE "major," minor	Int'l Stu Minor, $$, Resume	Graduation requirement	Major, HASS, Int'l Stud	Job prep, $$	Major req, Thesis work	Major & Master req, publish
Class 2	Chemistry 1			MechE Contrls 1	Manuf'g 1		Electoral Politic	Polisci Lab	Go to China!	Quant Methods	Chinese Frg'n Pol
Benefits	Graduation req "major"			MechE "major," minor	MechE "major," minor		Polisci Mjr, Field Req'mt	Major req, Thesis work	Rewarding, "job prep"	Major & Master req, Thesis work	Master req, "job prep"
Class 3	Physics 1	Physics 2		Weapons systm	US Military Pwr		Frgn Policy Thry	Chinese IV		Great Pwr Milit'ry	Nuke Forces in IR
Benefits	Graduation req	Grad req		Polisci "Minor," HASS" Mjr	Polisci "Minor," HASS" Mjr		Polisci Mjr, Master, Thesis	HASS, Int'l Stud Minor		Major & Master, "job prep"	Master req, "job prep"
Class 4	Calculus 1	Causes of War		Tech Pub Policy	Tech in History		Polisci Methods	Chinese E Asia		Mid East Conflict	IR Thry Seminar
Benefits	Graduation req	Polisci "Minor," HASS" Mjr		Polisci "Minor," HASS" Mjr	HASS (wasted)		Polisci Mjr, Thesis	HASS, Int'l Stud Minor		Major & Master, "job prep"	Master req, "job prep"
Class 5	(18 AP Credits)	(Calculus 2)		(Meche Tools)			Chinese III			Bioethics	
Benefits	(extra cred from APs)	(Eng. Prereq; January Term)		(MechE "Mjr," mnr, Jan term)			HASS'mt, Int'l Stud Mnr			(Thesis Work) (Done during January Term)	Major "field" req (January Term)
EC 1	Rugby	Flag Football	Gym	Frisbee	Gym	Gym	Gym	Gym	Gym	Research Job 2	Research Job 2
Benefits	Fitness, fun	PE Reqm't, Fitness	Fitness	PE Req'mt, Fitness	PE Req'mt, Fitness	Fitness	PE Req'mt, Fitness	PE Req'mt, Fitness	Fitness	Publish, $$, reccomendation	Publish, $$, recommendation
EC 2	Compsci Resrch	MIT Robo Team	MIT Robo Team	MIT Robo Team	Research Job 1		Dorm VP	Dorm VP		Research Job 3	Research Job 3
Benefits	$$, Compsci exploration	Explore, "Mech Experience"	Explore, "Mech Experience"	Explore, "Mech Experience"	Int'l Stu Minor, $$, Resume		Rewarding, resume	Rewarding, resume		$$, resume, recommendation	$$, resume, recommendation
EC 3	MIT Race Team			UA Senate	UA Senate		Frat Council	Frat Council			
Benefits	Explore, "Mech Experience"			"Rewarding," resume	"Rewarding," resume		Rewarding, resume	Rewarding, resume			

Noteworthy, by Semester

Freshman	Sophomore	Junior	Senior
-Declared Computer Science Major -Chose Political Science as Humanities Focus	-Declared Mechanical Engineering Major -Declared MechE + CompSci "Robo" Major -Chose Polisci as Minor -"Technology in History" ultimately wasted due to bad planning	-Declared Political Science Major (fell in love) -Declared MechE Minor -New humanities focus necessary (could not be my major)--Chose Chinese Studies -Declared Int'l Studues (China) Minor -Chose my Thesis--used 3 classes to work on it	-Got approval for Masters Degree -Used 2 classes to work on thesis

Example 4: A More Ideal College Schedule

For illustration of the power of good planning up front, I want to show how the schedule could have looked, had I planned it "perfectly" from the beginning. To be honest, plans will rarely be perfect: something will go wrong, you'll have a revelation, et cetera. That's fine. I got very lucky that mine worked out despite poor planning, and I want to show you how much "breathing room" you get by planning better.

This plan takes seven semesters. If I want to stay for eight? Great! I can relax, cut to four classes/semester after the first, and either cut some January Term classes or add really rewarding stuff throughout. I would probably stay pretty aggressive and leave the last term for "breathing room" or a bunch of fun classes not required for graduation.

Notes about this plan:

» Because I'm not omniscient, this still has me explore Computer Science & Mechanical Engineering

» I don't succumb to laziness—I test out of Calc I and Physics I

» Same number of five-class terms (two)

» Still assumes I still want to keep the Political Science Master's

» "Sneer quotes" indicate that a class or activity didn't have the intended effects. For example: if a class has a note saying "minor," it means I intended (at the time of taking) for it to contribute to a minor but it ended up not doing so.

A More Ideal College Schedule

Classes & Benefits	Freshman			Sophomore			Junior			Senior	
	Semester 1	Semester 2	Summer 1	Semester 3	Semester 4	Summer 2	Semester 5	Semester 6	Summer 3	Semester 7	Semester 8
Class 1	Physics 2	Diff Equations	Better intern	MechE Ctrls 2	Chinese IV	Research Job 1	Mid East Conflic	E Asia Int'l Rel'n	Consult Intern	Thesis Proposal	
Benefits	Grad req'mt, Eng. Prereq	Eng. Prereq	Something not compsci :)	MechE Minor round-out	HASS'mt, Int'l Stud Mnr	Int'l Stu Minor, $$, Resume	Master, "job prep"	Major, HASS, Int'l Stud	Job prep, $$	Major req, Thesis work	
Class 2	Intro Compsci	MechE Cntrls 1		Tech Pub Policy	Biology 1		Electoral Politic	Polisci Lab		Great Pwr Mil	
Benefits	Compsci major explore	MechE major explore		Polisci "Minor," HASS" Mjr	Graduation Requirement		Polisci Mjr, Field Req'mt	Major req, Thesis work		Major & Master, "job prep"	
Class 3	Calculus 2	Manuf'g 1		Weapons systm	Frgn Policy Thry		Quant Methods	Nuke Forces in IR		Thesis	
Benefits	Grad req'mt, Eng. Prereq	MechE major explore		Polisci "Minor," HASS" Mjr	Polisci Mjr, Master, Thesis		req, Thesis work	Master req, "job prep"		Major & Master req, publish	
Class 4	MechE Statics 1	US Military Pwr		Chinese IV	Polisci Methods		Bioethics	Chinese E Asia		Chinese Frg'n Pol	
Benefits	MechE major explore	Polisci Minor, HASS'mt		HASS, Int'l Stud Minor	Polisci Mjr, Thesis		Major "field" req	HASS, Int'l Stud Minor		Master req, "job prep"	
Class 5	(MechE Tools)	Causes of War	[18 AP Credits]	(Chemistry 1)			(Chinese V)	IR Thry Seminar		(Thesis Work)	
Benefits	MechE major, January Term	Polisci "Minor," HASS" Mjr	(extra cred from APs)	(Grad req'mt, January term)			(Fun! January term)	Master req, "job prep"		(Done during January Term)	
EC 1	Rugby	Flag Football	Gym	Gym	Frisbee	Gym	Gym	Gym	Gym		
Benefits	Fitness, fun	PE Reqm't, Fitness	Fitness	PE Req'mt, Fitness	PE Req'mt, Fitness	Fitness	PE Req'mt, Fitness	PE Req'mt, Fitness	Fitness		
EC 2	Compsci Resrch	MIT Robo Team	MIT Robo Team	UA Senate	Research Job 1		Dorm VP	Dorm VP	Research Job 2	Research Job 3	
Benefits	$$, Compsci exploration	Explore, "Mech Experience"	Explore, "Mech Experience"	"Rewarding," resume	Int'l Stu Minor, $$, Resume		Rewarding, resume	Rewarding, resume	Publish, $$, recommend'n	$$, resume, recommendation	
EC 3	MIT Race Team			Debate Team	Debate Team		Frat Council	Frat Council	Research Job 3	Research Job 2	
Benefits	Explore, "Mech Experience"			Rewarding, key skills	Rewarding, Key Skills		Rewarding, resume	Rewarding, resume	$$, resume, recommend'n	Publish, $$, reccomendation	

Noteworty, by Semester

- Test out of Physics 1 and calculus I
- Decide to test Compsci, Polici, and MechE as potential majors
- Only grad reqs are also eng. prereqs
- Decide from bad 1st term not to do Compsci
- Decide from experience to declare Polisci?

- Declared Mechanical Engineering Minor (take another class here to finish the minor)
- Choose Polisci as Major
- Choose my Thesis after Sophomore Fall
- New hum'ties focus--Choose Chinese Studies
- Declared Int'l Studues (China) Minor

- Get approval for Masters degree

- Finish thesis in January term after fall term--graduate in February

A Parting Thought

You don't have to get a Master's or double-major or any of that. If you want to, it's very possible if you plan well. If you don't, you can see above that graduating on time (or early!) is much less daunting, with the right approach.

All right! Wipe the sweat off your brow and pat yourself on the back—you've got a better career plan than perhaps all of your friends and peers.

It's time now to start thinking about how to effectively execute on the plan. You've got classes and extracurricular activities planned for each semester; in the next chapter, we're going to make sure it all goes as smooth as butter.

The Semesterly Picture

CHAPTER 3 CRUSHING EACH SEMESTER

Frequency: *every semester*

Total time: *a full working day (estimated)*

Tools: *your preferred calendar app (Google Calendar, iCal, Outlook, Thunderbird, etc), Crush College Career Planner (for reference; available at http://www.crush-college.com/tools)*

All right: We have a very high-level plan of how we want to use our college careers, and we have an idea of what we want to accomplish each semester. Now we want to go through the process of building a very robust plan for the semester—right at the beginning—that sets us up to really crush it. What we're going to have at the end of this chapter is a *really* thorough calendar that guarantees we'll not only know when to show up, but when to work on which parts of our assignments or projects. We'll have a predictable, spread-out flow of work that sets up to avoid the waste of confusion, a painful "crunch" at mid-term weeks, and confluences of multiple projects at once.

The basic sections:

    A. **Breaking Big Projects into Chunks**

    B. **Building Project Roadmaps**

    C. **Adding Everything to the Calendar**

The schedule should be updated as necessary, but we'll be looking at it at least every week, which means we're baking in some flexibility and making time to challenge its effectiveness.

A.   Breaking Big Projects into Chunks

"Write 40-page paper on Shakespeare" is a pretty daunting task. Just looking at the assignment makes me procrastinate. When something is either big or vague, it makes it both psychologically and tactically more difficult to approach. By breaking it down into chunks, we're able to work on a chunk at a time, knowing that completing that chunk successfully will mean we're on the path to success. It'll also help us avoid doing wasted work on the project, both by not doing chunks that we don't have to do and by not having to figure out what we're doing every time we sit down to work. Finally, it gives us some short-term pressure to get the chunk done. We humans work *really* well with deadlines, which is why we seem to get superhuman amounts of work done. The opposite of this principle is Parkinson's Law, in which "work expands to consume the time allotted to it." By allotting small chunks of time to small bits of work, we encourage the former and stave off the latter, which will naturally make us more productive when we are working.

We should go through this exercise for any project that's designed to take more than a week, including design projects, papers, lab experiments, art projects, et cetera[1].

Step by Step:

1. **Define the scope of the project with fine granularity**. We can also call this step, "understand the expectations and criteria for success to a high degree of detail." If a professor asks you to answer a certain question about history, you could write a two-page article or a tome without further guidance. How "strong" does the answer need to be? Often, a page count will be provided, and that should give you some sense of strength and thoroughness that's expected. But ask further interrogative questions: will you be expected to present counter-arguments and then eliminate them? What kind of "audience" are you writing for (layman or expert)? Are we trying to simply explain an event, figure out someone's motivations, or defend a general law of cause and effect? All these will change what your final work is going to look like. Engineers should know this process well, as should experimental scientists.

---

1   Once again I believe that there is great resistance to trying to "plan out" art or science experiments. In art, you "cannot direct the artistic process," and in science, you "cannot predict when a breakthrough will happen." My response is "tell that to your professor." Hate to break it, but you've got deadlines and thus limited time to do something. Given that, making a plan—*even if imperfect*—will only give you a leg up.

2. **Define what the end product should look like with similar detail**. Once we know the expectations, we can start defining the end product. For a theory paper, this may start by defining our paper as having a main thesis, three supporting arguments, two strong case-studies, and a refutation of alternative explanations for those cases. We can lay out the framework of the paper, we can define how many citations we will need for each part of this paper[2], et cetera.

3. **Plan backwards what "tasks" this will require at a high level**. For this, we're going to open Gantter, which is a free online "project-building" application. This is going to help us to continue this work in the next section, "Building Project Roadmaps."

   Here you might not yet know what your main argument (or final design) is going to be. That's fine. For now, we should have a sense of—for the example of a paper—how many pages we need to write, how many articles we need to read, et cetera. Build out these tasks in *reverse* order, starting from the end product and going "upstream" to the beginning. The more complex the project, the more closely you should follow these reverse planning steps:

   a) **Determine what immediate results (that is, closely and directly linked) the end product depends upon in order to be accomplished successfully**. For example, you may have an experimental report that requires some standard sections (hypothesis, field research, methodology, et cetera) you've defined in the previous step. For each of these sections, you'll have dependencies that include the writing and review; some will include the result of the experiment, others the field research.

   b) **For each earlier result, iterate writing the dependencies until you get back to the most basic steps you need in the project**. For the "experimental results" dependency of your report, you need your experimental design, materials, use of the right machines or space, etc. The experimental design requires a hypothesis, which requires an interesting question. Using the right machines may require training, gaining permission, or scheduling.

   Here's the experimental report dependency example illustrated:

---

2   A note on citations: I usually believe the number of necessary or helpful citations is *far less* than most students believe, and that they waste huge amounts of time stacking their paper with citations to either prove they've done research or show that lots of scholars agree. Your argument should stand strongly on its own and—I think—only need citations to prove out facts, to provide optional elaboration if you're quickly summarizing a principle or theory, and to cite *counter-arguments* that you're refuting. That's it. Your professors can smell fear and they can smell bullshit.

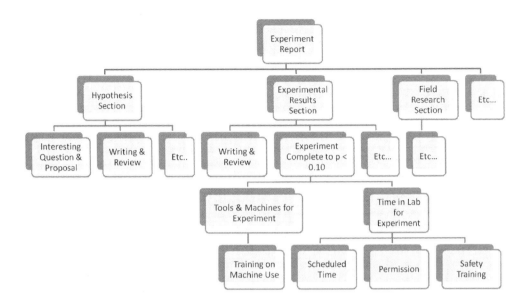

This can be done on paper (which is what I do) or in Gantter. You don't actually need to list steps in chronological order—putting in the start/stop dates will automatically sort them into chronological order for you.

c) Pick your "main thrust" as early as possible. For a paper, this should mean picking your main thesis either right away (if you've already done background reading in class) or after a single article that presents both sides of the argument (even Wikipedia is valid for this purpose). For a design project, it should be a vision of the function and form. For an experiment, it should be the specific hypothesis. Without this decisive choice, people often get into paralysis or change their mind frequently and waste time.

d) Don't plan for more than you need. If $p < 0.05$ is good enough, don't get a sample size that's planning for $p < 0.001$. If a single history of an event gives you the facts you need to make your own interpretation, then don't plan to read three of them. Don't spend time on making diagrams beautiful or getting laminated covers for your paper. Don't make a fourth draft of a paper unless a professor tells you the paper is junk. You get the idea: 80/20 rule applies here. And what if you under-planned? It's no fun having to do more than you planned, but if you plan for too much, I pretty much guarantee you'll do so. So planning for less time makes it more likely we'll get the results in less time, and that's what matters.

4. **Make sure nothing's missing.** Did you remember to add time to build an outline and bibliography? Lab space setup and cleanup? You may have already nailed all this: if so, read on.

5. **Break these tasks down to take no longer than a day.** You may have a 25-page paper to write. Realistically, how many pages will you write per day once you've got your citations, notes, and outline done? This will depend on how many hours per day you'll be dedicating per day. If you want to stay sane, I don't recommend more than six or so. This would mean 10-12 pages for me (before revisions, which is another day), but it may vary for you. Same goes for reading. The reason we do this is so that we have daily targets to help us know if we're on track.

6. **Fill in the details once you have your "main thrust" determined.** For now, you'll have some placeholders like "read article for first argument" or similar if you don't have your main thesis figured out yet. When you do have it figured out, fill in the details of your plan. Identify your main arguments. Quickly review some abstracts to determine what books or articles you'll need to read to support those (need inspiration? Wikipedia! It sometimes points to great sources—albeit sometimes to junk ones). All this will help you not only know what to do, but give you a better idea of how long each part will take: if you need to read a whole book rather than just a few chapters or an article, if you need to perform experiments that give results in two weeks rather than a day, or if you'll be creating six major features for your code rather than three[3].

Now we should have a task list in an approximately chronological order. Below is an example, in Gantter, of an article I'm planning to write on the causes of the Great Depression.

---

3 Frankly, I try to know the main thrust of a paper or experiment as soon as it's assigned. Usually it's related to previous class work, and I have strong opinions. Going for a topic related to class work also means you've done much of the background reading and should already have notes and some citations ready to go, as well as some supporting arguments.

Example 1: A Sample Research Paper into Chunks

 Great Depression Paper

Project   Edit   View   Actions   Extensions   Help   Autosave: OFF

Tasks

Resources

Calendars

#	Name	Duration
1	Read Wikipedia article on Causes of Great Depression	1d?
2	Decide whether to support Keynes or Hayek	1d?
3	Find P/E ratios, wages, interest rates, consumer spending in 1920s	1d?
4	Read Mises's "Theory of Money and Credit" section on boom/bust	1d?
5	Read Keyenes' "Economic Consequences of the Peace" on boom/bust	1d?
6	Collect notes & write outline	1d?
7	Write pages 1-6	1d?
8	Write pages 7-12	1d?
9	Write pages 11-16	1d?
10	Build bibliography	1d?
11	Revise into second draft	1d?
12	Trade with friend for proofreading	1d?
13	Third and final draft	1d?

We'll fill in durations later

Only historical data I need

I need to know both in order to support one and refute other

B.   Building Project Roadmaps

Now that we have our list of steps, we're going to assign dates to each of them so we know when to do them. Once again, we're going to plan backwards and give ourselves plenty of time, starting early and building in buffer space.

The challenge here is determining "how long will a step take?"—that is, how many hours. Sadly, there is no rule of thumb. First, it depends on the scope of the task (are you reading a whole bloody book or the key parts of it?). After that, it's your working speed. Increasing focus and eliminating distraction (in Part IV) will reduce this time and you'll work faster than you have in the past. But ultimately this working pace will vary for everyone. You'll need to depend in part on experience from high school. Like most things in life, the first time you do this, you'll suck at it, and you'll get better with time. Don't sweat it too much—having even a mediocre plan beats the pants off having none.

Step by step:

1. **Add the due date and give yourself a safety margin.** You can add "finish" dates to Gantter. If you make the duration zero days, it becomes a milestone; do this to your due date. For your last task before the due date, give yourself some buffer: a few days or a week[4].

2. **Check that everything in your list of tasks requires a day, unless you're not the one doing it.** If you're waiting for feedback, for example, it can be as many days as you'll need to wait[5]. Divide everything else (based on the number of hours you intend to spend on it per day) Into one-day tasks.

3. **Set up the predecessors, end to beginning.** Starting with your last task, set up the immediate predecessor for each task. Depending on how you've written your tasks, you may have simultaneous tasks (day-long centrifuge and writing the experimental methodology section). These simultaneous tasks should have the same predecessor and should both be predecessors for the next task.

4. **Create gaps where appropriate.** I prefer not to work on papers during the weekend (though some people like to dedicate a Sunday and end up doing the equivalent of two weekdays' work—whatever works for you). I may also have gaps in areas where I know I have some other major commitment coming up.

5. **Iterate your gaps during section C.** When your calendar fills up, you may find that you're doing way too much work in some weeks and not enough in others. We can create gaps in these projects so they avoid mid-term weeks, vacation weeks,

---

4   Gantter has a good video for first-time users that will cover how to do all of this: http://gantter.com/help/videos

5   Tip: when asking for advice, agree beforehand when you'll get it back.

conferences, or anything else where one might be pretty slammed with work. This just means starting earlier.

There are other clever things you can do with Gantter that can either add to the clarity of your chart or just add bureaucracy, depending on what works for you. I've only included what I think you really need; some people will use "indenting" tasks (under "Actions") to create larger task groups. These groups might be labeled "thesis selection," "research," "outlining," "writing," "revising," etc. I think it's unnecessary unless your project is absolutely gigantic.

As you prefer, you can add colors for clarity, "resources" (or task owners, for group projects), and multiple parallel parts (if you're spending some time waiting for a biology experiment to grow and want to write your methodology section in parallel, for example). You can share it and it just sits on the cloud. All in all, Gantter is a good app without too many bells and whistles.

Example 2: A Sample Research Paper in Project Roadmap Form

Here's my Great Depression paper with the dates and predecessors added. This example's pretty simple.

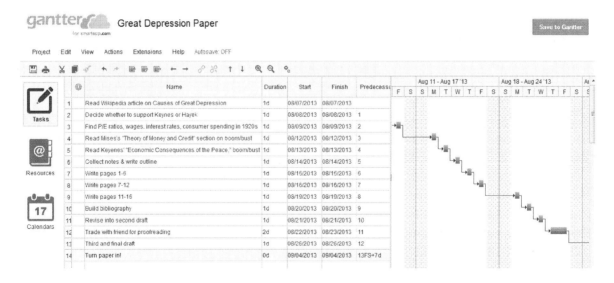

C.   Adding Everything to the Calendar

I have some friends that swear by college scheduling apps that act as a separate calendar for classes and homework, along with reminders about when assignments are due. Having tested them out myself, I am quite certain that they have no features of import beyond what you can get from Google Calendar, iCal, Outlook, Thunderbird, etc. In reality, your college schedule should go in whatever calendar you use for everything else: your life includes both your classes and a whole lot else. I suspect there will be (and maybe are) some schools that have schnazzy apps in which one simply enters the classes one is taking in a semester and it exports everything relevant to your calendar apps, contacts, etc. Unless and until those exist, we're doing it the old-fashioned way!

This is a pretty simple process, but it is going to be thorough. We're adding *everything* we know of to our calendar: classes (when and where to show up), homework assignments, major projects, major tests, sports practices, dance classes, whatever. There will be gaps that we fill in on a weekly basis (who knows what your second Saturday in November will look like when thinking about it in August?), and there will be some weekly recurring stuff that doesn't have a pre-set time (like email, or shopping for food), so we won't worry about those for now.

Step by Step:

1. **Get your classes into your schedule**. Look up what times they are every week— add them for a single week and then you can ask your calendar app to have weekly recurrence for all the weeks in the semester. Some advice on this:

   a) Make your class schedule its own "sub-calendar" that can be viewed on its own, with its own color

   b) Add the classrooms to your classes

   c) Find days and weeks off in your school's semesterly calendar and adjust yours

   d) If you need reminders to get your butt in gear, add them, perhaps for 15 minutes or however long it's going to take you to haul yourself to your class. Most calendar apps will show up on your phone and that can remind you if you're the forgetful type.

2. **Add exams and homework assignments**. Add when assignments are due to the hour—I've made the mistake of handing in an assignment late because I only knew the day, even though I'd finished it 3 days before. Similarly, I suggest assignments having their own sub-calendar. Have reminders for these a few days in advance in case you totally blow it during your weekly planning[6].

---

6   For exams and short assignments, I add "study for X" or "do calculus p-set 3" to the "all day" or "tasks" (depending on preference) part of the calendar for all of two, three, and four days beforehand so there's no chance of me panicking at the end.

3. **Add other recurring appointments**. Dance class, sports practice and meets... you get the idea. Look to your "Weekly Pursuits" page in the Crush College Career Planner for the important stuff.

4. **Add any other events**. Vacations, conferences, other travel, parties you know of ahead of time. Make sure you've recorded action for as many of your selected goals as you can. We want to get as on-top-of-things as possible.

5. **Export your projects from Gantter to your calendar**. By clicking "project" and selecting "export to calendar," you can choose from among a number of different calendars (iCal, Google Calendar, and any other calendar that can import from a URL) for your project to magically appear on your calendar. Just check beforehand that it's not going to collide with anything already in your calendar before you do so.

6. **Spread things out as appropriate**. If all your P-Sets are due Monday, then do some early in the week, some late—just change the recurring time each week. If you have three papers to write, you can either do them all at once (each taking three times as long) or do them in series. I prefer doing them in series as it's easier to juggle the concepts of one paper in my head, rather than three.

At this point, you've got an excellent schedule. Now: I'm asking you to start projects early, rather than right at the end. For many people, this is new territory and psychologically difficult. If you *prefer* a few all-nighters in a row before mid-term week, that's fine... but I don't think most people actually do. Procrastinating is a natural human thing (see my note earlier about "Parkinson's Law"), so we have to think of our schedules above as self-imposed deadlines. For how to actually stick to these, see Part III, "Staying On Track and Focused."

The Weekly Picture

CHAPTER 4 CRUSHING EACH WEEK

Frequency: *every week*

Total time: *20-40 minutes*

Tools: *Your preferred calendar app*

I used to be fairly averse to planning every bloody week. Couldn't I use that half hour to hour for something else? Maybe more Youtube? In my nobler moments I believed I was honestly too busy (especially before finals week). Every time I failed to do it, I regretted it. It's a very simple process, so I want to focus this chapter primarily on *why it's so important*. The weekly plan:

> » **Saves anxiety and enables focus.** One of the biggest focus-killers is the distraction of anxiety in your own mind. Ever had trouble working on project A because you're worried about other junk, or do you find yourself having moments of clarity that something was forgotten, then dropping everything to go do it? When we plan our week in detail, we make sure everything has a place and a time to be done. With a good plan, our present selves can trust our past selves to have made sure that we can presently focus and that, by following the plan, we'll succeed.

> » **Saves confusion and "switching time."** When you know precisely what you need to do next, you can crack open whatever it is and hop to it, rather than stepping back every time you finish something and deciding what to do next. It also helps you make sure in the morning that you're prepared for everything coming up

that day, rather than depending on luck. This alone is worth way more than the 40-minute weekly investment.

» **Enables micro-efficiency**. Planning transit or other low-productivity periods means we'll be able to squeeze something useful out of them rather than sit around like cows in a pasture. (Part III will have more on micro-efficiency.)

» **Sets you up to re-organize on the fly**. Also in Part III, daily execution requires being flexible, as "no plan survives contact with the enemy." But by all means, this does not mean one should not plan, but that one should have a plan he or she can alter at any point. Without a weekly plan, a wrench in the works means chaos; with one, you can re-shuffle the calendar in a few minutes. As General Dwight D. Eisenhower, representing even the most hardcore plan-haters, said: "for battle, I have always found that plans are useless but planning is indispensable."

It's a good thing. We're not trying to lock you in a schedule-cage like some kind of man-imal, just make sure you're able to avoid wasting time and spend it doing what you really want to. Just try it. The order below is designed to have you move from those things more strictly scheduled to those with more flexibility.

Step by Step:

1. **Review the schedule you set at the beginning of the schedule and move or add anything obvious**. Things change: you drop classes, snow days happen, et cetera. Look first at what's already scheduled and make sure it's valid.

   a) Make sure all of your classes, sports, projects, club meetings, et cetera, are there.

   b) Add any events that came up recently, like party or dinner invitations, talks by your favorite speakers, or anything else of interest.

2. **Add life maintenance**: Schedule sleep, morning preparations, prep for night, meals, laundry, food shopping, and anything else along these lines.

3. **Add non-scheduled work**: For work on longer projects, normal assignments, reading, labs, etc: you already know what days you'll be doing the work from your project roadmaps. Here, place the work into free spots in the schedule with an eye to the environment you'll be in (e.g.: can you easily access a computer?), in two- to three-hour blocks of time. If you find shorter or longer blocks improve your concentration and flow, do it later, but start with two to three hours for now. We'll cover more on adjusting these time blocks in Part III.

On estimating time: like in your semesterly plans, you are likely going to have some anxiety at estimating how much time something is going to take. How much time is required for that math P-Set, that design exercise, that reading assignment, that section of the paper? It's tough, and sadly there's no easy answer. My gut has gotten better in time, as will yours. What I suggest for your first weeks is this:

a) **Plan each time block aggressively.** Give yourself time blocks that make you a bit uncomfortable. This "worry" about whether we'll get it all done in time has been shown to make us work a lot faster. If you don't make it at first, that's okay, because you should also...

b) **Plan some goof-off time near the end of the** day: It should be optional but fairly exciting. Maybe it's video games or pleasure reading or a movie. Don't schedule something you're socially obligated to go to, but if you're looking forward to it, it will motivate you in the earlier work blocks to stay on top of it. But should your estimates be over-ambitious, leftover work can eat into this time without disastrous consequence.

After a few weeks of that practice, you should be able to hone in your estimation accuracy, and you can repeat the above practice in times of doubt. My grave warning here is to not get lazy and schedule too much time for anything, as Parkinson's Law[1] will take effect.

4. **Add other weekly goals.** Go back to your "Weekly Recurring" tab in the Crush College Career Planner and make sure any goals that made it to that list are covered appropriately in your weekly plan.

5. **Add time for email and your to-do list.** I usually give them a total of an hour combined each day; sometimes this is going to go up.

6. **Use extra time at discretion.** All right! You've got your school work, appointments, personal projects, sleep, social time, and pretty much everything else in the schedule. Still time left? Use it at your discretion! I like to leave some "goof off" time as a buffer in case I get into long conversations with friends or inspiration strikes for me to draw or write.

If you consistently have a lot of leftover time... then consider whether it's time to look to an item in your force-ranked hierarchy of goals and add the next-highest one that doesn't have any (or much) time devoted to it. Do what you will, but don't persistently waste your own time. There's a huge difference between "relax-

---

1   "All work expands to fill the time allotted to it," or other phrasings.

ation time" and "dead time" or "a few hours on Facebook" time. Don't mistake one for the other!

Example 1: Book Draft Deadline Week's Calendar

The following example is from the craziest week of my summer in Europe: trying to get my first draft of Crush College out for review while visiting Berlin. I did squeeze some of it near the end because I knew the "itch" of seeing lots of Berlin in my first week there would be just too much for me to be able to concentrate. A few notes:

» To-do list and social media junk were in the morning after my first block of work

» Working out is in there before breakfast

» I still got 7-9 hours of sleep each night

Other than that, it's busy and full of lots of fun with the Berliner friends we made while we were there. (I've omitted a few details for simplicity and privacy.)

The only other thing worth noting is that this deadline is self-imposed, but I was still motivated to hit it because I'd promised about seven people that I'd get them a copy by Friday evening, and that I'd owe them each a 12-pack of their favorite beer if I was late. That's 84 beers! Very motivating! More on this in, of course, Part IV, "Staying On Track and Focused."

Calendar

CREATE

August 2013

S	M	T	W	T	F	S
28	29	30	31	1	2	3
4	5	6	7	8	9	10
11	12	13	14	15	16	17
18	19	20	21	22	23	24
25	26	27	28	29	30	31
1	2	3	4	5	6	7

My calendars
- Work Misc
- Book
- Social
- Summer Fun

Other calendars
- Add a friend's calendar
- Anton Life Schedule

nptvoid(0); davs

Aug 4 – 10, 2013

GMT-05

Time	Sun 8/4	Mon 8/5	Tue 8/6	Wed 8/7	Thu 8/8	Fri 8/9	Sat 8/10
(all day)			Jazz			FIRST DRAFT	Cheat Day / Tiergarten Quella
1pm							1:30p – 6p Tour Art Museums, TV Tower
2pm	2p – 3p Lunch & Email	2p – 3p Lunch & Email	2p – 3p Lunch & Email	2p – 3p Lunch & Email	2p – 3p Lunch & Email	2p – 3p Lunch & Email	
3pm	3p – 5p Book: Find Gantt Tool?	3p – 5p Book: Cheat Sheets 4 – 5	3p – 5p Book Block: S4.1	3p – 5p Book Block: S2.1	3p – 5p Book Block: S2.2	3p – 6p Final Review	
5pm	5p – 6p German Lesson 9	5p – 6p German Lesson 10	5p – 6p German Lesson 11		5p – 6p German Lesson 13		
6pm	6p – 7:30p Book Block: S1.3	6p – 7:30p Book Block: S1.4	6p – 7p Book Block Cheat Sheet 3	6:30p – 8p Get Food & Cook	6p – 7:30p Book Block: S2.3	6p – 7p Format & Send Outl...	6:30p – 8:30p Dinner @ TG Quella
7pm			7:30p – 9p Cook & Eat			7p – 8p German Lesson 14	
8pm	8p – 12 Movie & Thai Night	8p – 10p Dinner w/ Hosts		8p – 12 Csárka Paprikas Party	8p – 10p Cook & Eat Steak	8p – 9p Quick Dinner	
9pm			9p – 11:30p Jazz @ Edelweiss			9p – 12 Edelweiss	9p – 12 Kreuzberg & Clubs w/ Stephan
10pm		10p – 11:30p Nietzsche			10p – 12 Beergarden		

The Hourly Picture

CHAPTER 5: RUTHLESSLY ELIMINATING WASTE

Frequency: *occasionally; approximately every month*

Total time: *varies significantly; allot some 30 minutes per day for a few weeks for time studies or reinforcing some of the tougher habits*

Tools: *Crush College Timesheet Tool and Pareto Builder, Gantter, Crush College Prioritization Tool (available at http://www.crush-college.com/tools), others (chosen by you as appropriate; see below)*

Even within a good weekly plan, there's tons of wasted time that we can go after. This is great news; it means that even when we're operating at a much higher level than our past selves (or our peers), we can still do even better—meaning more time and more progress in your most important goals.

We can eliminate waste from any plan using the same principles. The process outlined below is general and the examples are of both a weekly routine and a year-long project.

Remember our fourth principle: **far more improvement is possible than you currently believe**. This is the step in our journey in which we transcend from being a great student to becoming a marvel for others, the student that mysteriously does it all and barely breaks a sweat.

Anticipate that it's possible to eliminate some 50% of the total time you spend on any one process. We won't go after all of it: our **80/20 principle** applies to this effort just like any other.

Effectively eliminating wasted time involves three steps:

A. **Identifying All Possible Wasted Time** in the process by getting strong facts

B. **Prioritizing Which Waste to Eliminate** next based on the **80/20 principle**

C. **Executing Top-Priority Recovery Projects** with the right tools

A) Identifying Wasted Time

To identify wasted time we must venture forth into our lives to determine either how much time we plan to spend doing something (for a project in the future) or how much time we currently use to perform a task (typically a routine that we repeat each day, week, etc).

This is where we depart from typical "time management" philosophy, which is based on tips, tricks, or habits that you "should" adopt. Instead, by identifying the biggest sources of wasted time, we will custom-tailor a few key tools that yield the biggest return. It's a beautiful thing.

There are two basic tools for identifying wasted time:

1. **SMED:** The term SMED comes from "Singe-Minute Exchange of Die," created by Toyota in the 1950s. Toyota wanted to reduce the total downtime on a milling machine when replacing a worn-down die, thereby increasing the cars per day they could make. They successfully (after many iterations) reduced the total down time by over 90% to fewer than 10 minutes (the "single" part of the name meaning "single digit"). It was such a huge success that it caught on in factories worldwide. We'll be using that same process to identify wasted time in any *repeated process* or any *project plan*.

2. **Time studies:** These are also used in factories but are incredibly applicable to business and life. Most generally, time studies are detailed recordings (often to the minute or to the second) of all time used in a particular process. A common example: one might stand next to a machine with a stopwatch to determine how much time it is spending jamming, changing between products, waiting for materials, and running "well." Factories use the data to determine what problems to attack to increase productivity. And—you guessed it—we'll be doing the same thing for ourselves. In our case, we'll use time studies to identify *wasted time within our weekly routines*.

SMED: Step by Step

Tools: *Gantter*

1. Choose either a large project (perhaps a final paper) or a repeated process (if you've identified a repeated process you want to shorten from your Time Study—perhaps your morning routine)

    a) If a *project*: pick the largest project in the upcoming semester that hasn't yet been improved. This could be a research paper, a lab project, design project, even an art project[1].

    b) If a *routine*: it should be a routine that occurs frequently and takes up a large amount of time in your week.

2. Build a *highly detailed* **schedule** of the project or routine in the Project Scheduling Tool (as discussed in "Breaking Big Projects into Chunks") with the appropriate granularity—that is, each step or task in the project should take one or more of the appropriate units of time. If some of your tasks take less time than your smallest time unit, then your units are too big. For any task of greater than a few units, challenge yourself to break it down into smaller chunks. The more detail you have, the more wasted time you'll see. Here are some suggested time units for different project or process lengths:

    a) Year or semester: to the week or day

    b) Month: to the day or working block (two to three hours)

    c) Day: to the five minute block

3. Create a **target** total time for the project. Base the target on accomplishing a discrete goal. Perhaps you want to shave three weeks off a paper to give you breathing space for another paper or a conference or a vacation (nobody wants to work over spring break!), or perhaps you want to cut half an hour out of your morning routine to get a half-hour more sleep.

4. Determine the **critical path**. The critical path is the set of steps such that, if you reduce the length of any, the whole project will get shorter. Steps *not* on the critical path are those that, if they get shorter, won't shorten the total project. For some projects, *everything* will be on the critical path in the first iteration of the plan, be-

---

1   I've found that the creative art majors tend to be most resistant to believing there is wasted time within the "creative process." Work with me here—at the very least, let's eliminate the time spent not being creative: the administrative or procedural stuff you need to do. But, ultimately, if you're attempting to improve a skill of any sort, there is a better way to do it and it's worth the research. More on this later.

cause nothing is being done in parallel. Some examples of stuff that will be done in parallel and not on the critical path:

a) The time it takes your laundry to dry if you're going to get it after class

b) Waiting for code to compile if you're able to work on other parts of a project while waiting

c) Running a lab machine for a few days while you work on the report

5. For each step/task, **ask the four questions of SMED** in order. This is the critical moment! Applying principle seven (vigorously challenge all assumptions and beliefs) will mean the difference between glorious victory and thinking all of this is a waste of time. At the end of the day it's up to you—I can't do the thinking for you and nor can anyone else. When you're asking these questions, remember that we're not only looking for wasted time that we can get rid of by snapping our fingers. We're looking for *all of it*—anything that can be improved by better methods. It'll take work to actually *make* the improvement and that shouldn't stop us from identifying it. Note that the questions are ordered such that the earlier questions are the most effective. Let's take a look:

a) **Does it need to be done at all?** Eliminate, automate, and outsource, my friend! You'd be shocked at just how much you do in a project or during the day that you just plain don't need to do. For *everything*, ask—does it directly further my goals? If so, can I automate it so I don't have to do it myself?

b) **Can I do it outside the cycle?** This is most relevant for projects, but applies to routines, as well. My favorite example of this is shamelessly using assignments and papers to lay the groundwork for a thesis, capstone project, et cetera. Much of the work is done "before you start."

c) **Can it be done sooner or in parallel?** There's a whole lot that can be done in parallel with other things (and thus taken out of the "critical path") that we don't take advantage of when we're not thinking. How about making sure you pre-heat the oven before starting to gather your materials for cooking? In projects and your daily routine, there are numerous opportunities to parallelize and get time back seemingly for free[2].

d) **Can it be done faster?** This doesn't necessarily mean running to class (but hey, maybe get a bike—it's good for you). This is often the improvement that takes the most creativity and work. Have you researched methods to

---

2   Note: this does not mean multi-tasking. Multi-tasking, or doing two things at once that *require your attention*, has been debunked a thousand times by very solid studies. Don't do it. If you do it, *stop* doing it.

improve skills (like speaking foreign languages, shooting free-throws, or playing flute) that you practice often? If your work require lots of reading, have you considered techniques for reading faster? How about reading less[3]? For each of these steps, look briefly on the Internet into what new methods promise and then choose a potential improvement ("20% faster" or similar) based on that.

6. **Challenge yourself**—what creative, daring, or disruptive potential solutions have you neglected? Get outside input. Remember we are not committing to doing all of this! We'll figure out what we do and what we don't later. However, don't neglect anything just because it's hard.

7. **Re-build the project with all the saved time**. To see the full savings potential, build a new file in Gantter, where all identified wasted time is eliminated.

8. List each step with how much total time can be saved to let you move on to **Prioritizing**.

Example 1: Erik's Master's Thesis (a Large Project)

My thesis is perennially my favorite example of how using a *smart process* made me look like superman—and impressed the heck out of peers, professors, and potential employers. The key takeaway here is that with the right creative, challenging look, the execution is a lot easier than you might think. Let's look at how I did it.

First, below is my original Master's thesis schedule (yes, it's simplified). I wasn't entirely sure how much I'd have to read, due to not having a topic at all… but I estimated. Remember the schedule can change as you learn more, but just having one is hugely helpful on its own. I *did* know it would be highly quantitative, thus the dataset/graphs. My original plan would take a year from when I started, but would ultimately mean going into a 9th semester, which would have been very expensive. So my goal was to cut total time in half.

Before you move on to see where I found improvement opportunity, I want you to use the SMED questions to find as much as you can. Jot down what you see and then move on.

---

3   You may have realized that "reading less" technically falls under the first question, but we put it here because it's too easy for the first question to make us think of "eliminating it altogether" rather than "part of it."

Task	Semester 1 Weeks														Semester 2 Weeks													
	1	2	3	4	5	6	7	8	9	10	11	12	13	14	1	2	3	4	5	6	7	8	9	10	11	12	13	14
Pick ideas	■																											
Wait: idea approval		■																										
Formal proposal			■																									
Create reading list				■																								
Read book 1					■																							
Read book 2						■																						
Read book 3							■																					
Read articles 1-6								■																				
Read articles 7-12									■																			
Code for dataset										■	■																	
Collect dataset												■																
Find correlations													■	■	■	■												
Build graphs																	■											
Write outline																		■	■									
Get feedback																				■								
Write draft 1																					■	■	■	■				
Get feedback																									■			
Final draft																										■	■	
Defend & Submit!																												■

Seriously, don't peek. The exercise is important.

Promise you've done the exercise? Great! Here's what I got. I'll add some detail below the image:

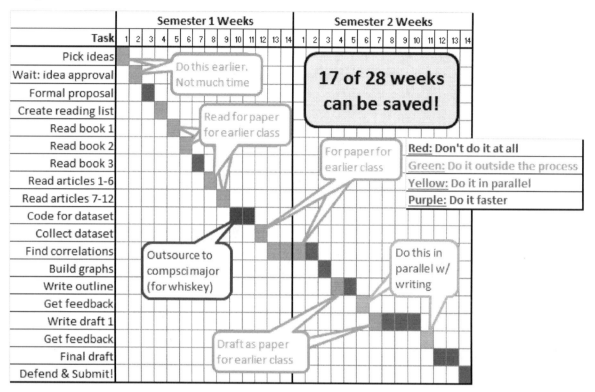

Picking my ideas and getting approval could be done very early—I finished at the end of my sophomore year so I could plan out the rest of it.

Once I had my idea, I *matched electives in my major to that idea*. Four classes focused either directly or indirectly on my thesis. They allowed me to:

» Do reading that related to my thesis, giving me the notes, insight, and citations I needed; and

» Write papers that would (potentially—some did, some didn't) constitute chapters of my thesis and make up a major part of the quantitative analysis.

» It was by planning in this way that all of the "green" blocks ("outside the cycle") came to be both planned and realized.

I also outsourced the code-writing to assemble my mega-dataset (which ended up being an obnoxious 600,000 data points). I did the analysis myself but building the dataset was a pain and (as we covered earlier) I lack these skills. In exchange, my good friend got whiskey and contributor status in the thesis. Took him a few hours where it would have taken me ages.

I also continued writing as I waited for feedback. No reason not to—I submitted the paper for feedback twice even when I knew there were some flaws that could be improved, which allowed me to keep working on it and not have to become idle[4].

The end result plan was below. It gave me a healthy buffer of three weeks to finish within that eighth semester. I did end up using that buffer for spring break (in which I didn't write at all) for a major overhaul requested by my advisor after the outline. But! It all worked out, I got my A, got a great recommendation, and disappointed my advisor by not publishing.

Task	Semester 1 Weeks														Semester 2 Weeks													
	1	2	3	4	5	6	7	8	9	10	11	12	13	14	1	2	3	4	5	6	7	8	9	10	11	12	13	14
Pick ideas																												
Wait: idea approval																												
Formal proposal	■																											
Create reading list																												
Read book 1																												
Read book 2																												
Read book 3		■																										
Read articles 1-6																												
Read articles 7-12																												
Code for dataset	■	■																										
Collect dataset																												
Find correlations			■																									
Build graphs				■																								
Write outline					■																							
Get feedback						■																						
Write draft 1							■	■																				
Get feedback								■																				
Final draft									■	■																		
Defend & Submit!												■																

Improvements like this can be made to many projects. I *didn't* consider how to write the drafts faster through learning how to type more quickly, but I *did* plan them aggressively ("Three weeks for a first draft!? Madness!" I hear you say) because I already knew how to keep out distraction and stay focused. We'll cover that more in Part IV, "Staying On Track and Focused."

---

4   This requires expectation management. When you submit for feedback, be clear on where you want and don't want feedback, "I haven't done a proofread yet, so don't worry about grammar" will prevent frustration on the part of your professor, TA, or other reader.

Time Study: Step by Step

Tools: *Crush College Time Study Tool, notebook and watch or Toggl, RescueTime*

The Time Study is going to be the part you'll most likely balk at doing. I won't lie: it's a pain in the ass tracking how you use your time. But holy smokes, it is worth it.

1. Determine a **period** to track your time (one week works)

2. Keep a *detailed* **account** of your time (snooze, shower, email, Facebook, transit, reading) in the Time Study Tool.

    a) First **list the different activities you perform during a day**. Get granular, to the level of "eat breakfast" and "shower," "check email," "date with boyfriend," etc. Try to get them in order. It won't be complete (and one-off activities will arise), but it'll be a good start. You'll pre-populate the recording tools you use.

    b) Here's the tough part! You're going to have to **keep track of how you use this time**, down to the five-minute block. Generally, computer and non-computer time can be tracked separately:

        i.   **For computer time**: there are a few great apps (the best is Rescue-Time[5]) that will *spy on you* and record which windows/programs you have open when your computer is on, and then give you a summary report. Be ready to for a few terrifying revelations. I use it every now and then just for a reality check.

        ii. **For non-computer time**: wear a watch, and bring a pocket note-book[6] and pen. Yup. To start just jot down the start/stop time of different activities[7]. Note when you wake up, when you get to your shower, when you start/stop breakfast, leave/arrive for class, etc. Get every five-minute block that you can; you really want more than 95% of time accounted for. It's going to be a pain in the butt for a week.

    c) **Record it in a central place**: It should take only about half an hour to re-cord your week's worth of date into the Time Study tool

---

5   https://www.rescuetime.com/tour_new
6   You could also use an app like Toggl (https://www.toggl.com/) to record this time but I have found the pocket notebook less intrusive and quicker to note.
7   For computer time, just jot down when you get onto and get off of the computer. Your recording app will take care of the rest.

3. Group times into appropriate **categories** (you might put Twitter, Facebook, and FourSquare into "Social Media") and build a **pareto** graph using the Time Study tool. This will show you the biggest categorical uses of your time.

4. For each bar, **find waste.** Not all time is wasted! For each category, time is either: completely wasted, partially wasted, or not wasted at all. Like in SMED, we use probing questions to hunt for waste within the time we're using in this order:

    a) **Can it go away?** (e.g.: cut out reddit, drop a club) Here's where it's key to have your goals nearby. For any activity that's not *very short*: does it contribute to these goals? If not, why the heck are you doing it? Mark it as wasted time and an opportunity to get more back.

    b) **Can it be automated?** (e.g.: automated bill-pay, peapod food delivery, etc) It's the future, hombre. If you don't know whether it can be automated, *it can be.* Google it, seriously. Know what's out there and see how much you could not be doing.

    c) **Can it be dramatically reduced?** (e.g.: Social media to 15 minutes per day or less?) Lots of stuff you can just *do less* of and not lose anything in your life, because it's just not that important. Again, check your goals.

    d) **Is it time you can use doing something else in addition?** (e.g.: reading on train, email while standing in line) This sometimes gets into "micro-efficiency" but there are often areas where you're "captive" and can do something else. Often these are times when you can't totally free your time but you can do the right work in addition, depending on context. For example, if you're ever driving and not listening to language lessons or audiobooks for class or personal improvement, you could use your time better[8].

    e) **Can you reduce frequency?** (batch cooking, laundry) Batching saves a lot of time. If I cook twice as much with 20% more cooking time, I'm winning. Think of repetitive tasks you can do less often, keeping the results "in storage." Take advantage of fridge space, laundry hamper space, etc. If it requires buying a few pair of socks to last into a second week, it may be worth it.

    f) **Can it be done faster?** (e.g.: improve focus with location, learn faster reading skills) This is where you have to get creative. Almost anything

---

8   You might insist here that music is critical to unwinding for you, which could be the case! But I encourage you to try out using this time for something higher on the priority list before you give up. I think people rarely say, "I wish I hadn't learned Chinese in the car." I also find "listening to the news" something that can be done in five minutes, rather than the whole car ride, so don't let that be an excuse.

you do can be done better, faster. The key principle here is the 5th: **rate everything you do in terms of results only**. Currently spending one hour per day on piano? You can either reduce that time or increase your results per hour through better techniques. There are no one-size-fits-all answers here[9], but I pretty much guarantee you can shave 20% off anything you do if you stay results-focused and do some research into more optimal techniques. We'll go over some techniques to improve focus in Part IV.

Here's what it looks like in the Time Study Tool:

Task	Avg Hrs/day	Task	Wasted hrs/day
Sleeping	5.8	Email	1.0
Sit in class	2.9	Walk to class	0.8
P-Set	2.6	P-Set	0.8
Class Reading	1.8	Class Reading	0.7
Email	1.6	Reddit	0.7
Socializing	1.6	Facebook	0.6
Reddit	0.9	Lunch	0.5
Facebook	0.8	Dinner	0.4
Walk to class	0.8	Cooking	0.3
Writing	0.6	Snooze	0.3
Cooking	0.6	Blogs/News	0.3
???	0.6	Writing	0.2
Blogs/News	0.5	Laundry	0.2
CompSci Lab	0.5	Groceries	0.1
Lunch	0.5	Webcomics	0.1
Shower	0.5	Sleeping	0.0
Dress	0.5	Sit in class	0.0
Dinner	0.4	Socializing	0.0
Laundry	0.4	???	0.0
Groceries	0.3	CompSci Lab	0.0
Snooze	0.3	Shower	0.0
Prep for bed	0.3	Dress	0.0
Webcomics	0.2	Prep for bed	0.0
Total	**25**	**Total**	**7.0**

5. **Challenge** yourself—what creative, daring, or disruptive potential solutions have you neglected?

---

9   The exception to this being Josh Kaufman's The First 20 Hours (http://first20hours.com/). Very much worth a read.

6. List each identified waste with total time. Update the **waste pareto** in the Time Study Tool.

You'll see some stuff that shocks you and some that will be so obvious as to be a headache. Some of it might be stuff that you've been fighting for a long time and given up on. This is all right—we're going to nail it because what we're doing is different from anything you've been taught before.

Example 2: Erik's Routine for a Week (Freshman)

This example of my freshman fall daily routine—where I slept little and still got nothing done—has been highly simplified, but still gets the point across. I didn't have fancy things like RescueTime or Toggle like you kids these days, but I recorded myself for two weeks and this was more-or-less what it looked like. Note the pareto below is 24 hours of time. The Time Study Tool will help you normalize your time into a day.

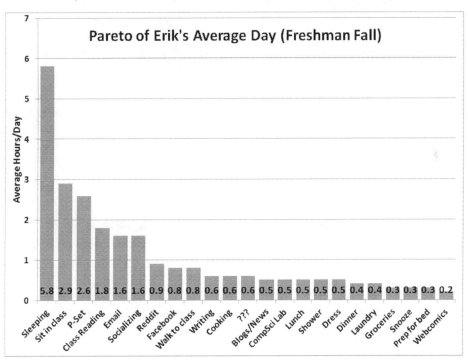

My goal at this point was to get to 7.5 hours/day of sleep (a luxurious five REM cycles) and get an extra hour and a half of time to work and stay on top of my game. If I could accomplish this, along with effective semester-level and weekly block planning, I would be in pretty good shape. (This was just the first round—I gutted a lot more time out of my schedule later in my college career.)

Like with the "thesis" example, don't move on until you've identified where I could recover time. Then we'll review what I got.

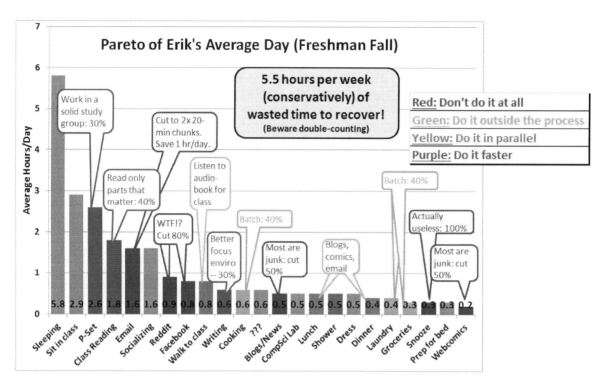

All right! Like before, I'll talk through what I found and why I believe it was there (or wasn't).

Here's what clearly wasn't wasted:

» Sleeping: I wanted *more* sleep!

» Sitting in class: There were classes in subsequent semesters where this was a waste of time, and so I would simply not show up to lectures—but not this semester. Not recommended as a default. Don't use this time as multi-tasking time, either: if it's not worth paying attention, it's not worth showing up.

» Socializing: I thought about the way I was using this time (good conversations with friends) and it was in sync with high-level goals for me. I didn't go to lousy parties, either.

» Shower, dress, bed: I had tried taking time out of these before and succeeded, but was pretty miserable. Decided it was time key to my sanity (a high-ranked goal).

» ???: I didn't know what this was because my recording was imperfect.

And here's where I found time could be recovered:

» P-Sets: I was in some bad study groups that slowed me down. Some others just shared answers and I had no interest in cheating. For some classes I joined new groups and others I did my work on my own, but I knew I could speed up.

» Reading: I often found myself reading stuff I knew was irrelevant. I knew I could skip chapters if I knew what the goal of the reading was.

» Email: I knew email distracted me and I got a lot of pretty low-quality mail. I knew mass unsubscriptions and selective responding was in my future.

» Reddit, Facebook, Blogs/News Webcomics: Just a distraction and mostly not adding to my life. Onto the wall for firing squad!

» Walking to class: I had a lot of walking and mostly jammed out. Realized I could listen to audiobooks of some of my class reading.

» Writing: I knew my focus was poor and there was opportunity improve it, even though I wasn't sure how.

» Cooking: I used to never make enough for leftovers. That could change quickly.

» Lunch and dinner: If I was eating alone I could read. If I was eating with others it was also socializing time[10].

» Laundry and groceries: cut frequency here in half as I had enough clothes and enough fridge space to do it.

» Snooze: turns out you don't actually get any more quality sleep from the extra 9 minutes (or 27 minutes of repeatedly waking up)—it's purely a waste of time[11].

Once I'd identified all the waste I could go after, I built a Pareto of the wasted time. It was fairly revealing about where the first projects might be.

---

10 At some point I quit trying to multi-task over meals—I started eating better food that was worth paying attention to and it became a goal for me to enjoy the food I was eating.

11 "Of course it is, but I can't help myself!" I hear you, friend. Be patient and read on to Section C. All will be revealed in time.

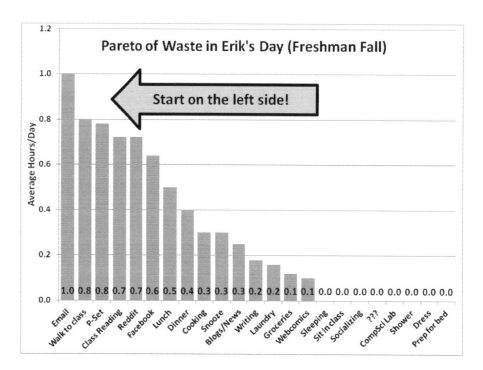

But going after all of this at once doesn't always make sense, and going after something "big" might not make sense if something else a bit smaller is *really easy*. Thus, we proceed to "B) Prioritization."

B)   Prioritizing Wasted Time

Tools: *Crush College Prioritization Tool*

With limited time and willpower available, we can only pursue one or a few recoveries at a time. We'll be going after the **most time recovered for the least effort** first. This means we might not go after the largest blocks of time first, if some slightly smaller ones are really easy.

I want to note that you might have wasted time that's *very obviously* worth going after immediately. If so, skip this step for now. This step is meant to help you pick what to go after first when you're in a target-rich environment. If you spend three hours per day on Facebook, *just go deal with that already* by skipping to "C) Executing Time Recovery Projects."

Prioritization: Step by Step

In the Prioritization Tool, for each identified wasted time item from your Time Study:

1. Write it as a **project** (e.g.: "reduce FOO by X%," "eliminate BAZ," etc) **with a targeted result**. That's because we're planning to *do something* about it. We might not know *how*—in fact, it's probably not useful to assume you know how unless it's bleedingly obvious. A good project name should thus not be "take Bob's class on writing" but "reduce writing time by 30%." Why? You might not want to *type faster* but instead just write or rewrite less. We're not sure yet.

2. Write the **approximate time it's worth** from your Time Study or SMED.

3. Determine the *relative* **difficulty to execute**, based on:

    a) Cost

    b) Time to implement

    c) Need for help from others

    d) Need to acquire a skill, gadget, product, et cetera

    e) Addition of "headache" to other parts of your life or erosion of other goals

   This is subjective but should be fact-based. Note that "I don't have the willpower to do it" is not a legitimate difficulty—we'll discuss the right techniques to stay motivated in Part IV. For now, consider only the above criteria when assessing the difficulty between any two projects.

4. Enter these values into the **Prioritization Tool**, which will auto-populate your priority chart:

    a) For time, enter the same units. Maybe "hours per day" for a routine or "days" for a project.

    b) For difficulty, simply put a 1-5 ("1" being easy and "5" being hard). Use the whole spectrum—it's all relative.

   Here's what it looks like in the Prioritization Tool:

Select units of time: | Hours

Project	Value (From Time Study or Gantter)	Difficulty (1 - 5; 1 is easiest)
Reduce Email	1	3
Read over Meals	0.9	2
Walk w/ Audiobook	0.8	3
Reduce Reddit	0.75	1
Reduce Facebook	0.65	1
Pset Study Group	0.5	3
Read Parts that Matter	0.4	4
Batch Cooking	0.3	2
Cut Snooze	0.3	1
Cut Blogs/News	0.25	1
Batch Laundry	0.2	2
Batch Shopping	0.15	2
Writing Focus	0.12	5
Reduce Webcomics	0.1	1

5. **Rank** the highest-priority projects that will let you meet your goal. These will be:

    a) Easiest to execute and

    b) Worth the most time.

6. **Choose** which projects to go after, based on your current improvement goals.

    Remember not to take on too much at once. If you're not sure, just do one at a time. The brain has some fundamental limits on how much it can effectively absorb or change at once.

7. Move on to **Execution**, where we decide how many to work on at once and how to lock them in.

Example 2: Prioritizing Erik's Weekly Routine Wasted Time

Remember that I wanted to get 7.5 hours of sleep and 1.5 more hours of work, which means I needed a total of **3.2 hours**. After using the Prioritization Tool, my projects looked like this:

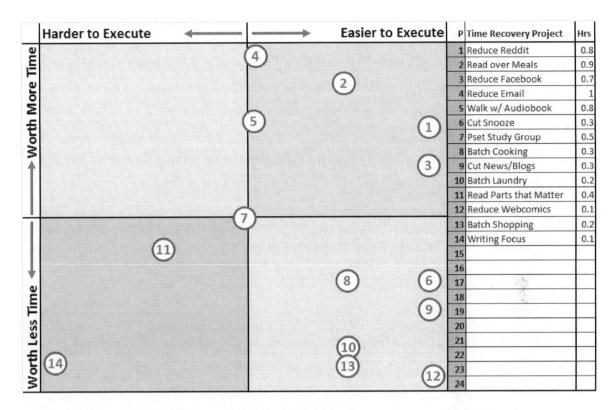

P	Time Recovery Project	Hrs
1	Reduce Reddit	0.8
2	Read over Meals	0.9
3	Reduce Facebook	0.7
4	Reduce Email	1
5	Walk w/ Audiobook	0.8
6	Cut Snooze	0.3
7	Pset Study Group	0.5
8	Batch Cooking	0.3
9	Cut News/Blogs	0.3
10	Batch Laundry	0.2
11	Read Parts that Matter	0.4
12	Reduce Webcomics	0.1
13	Batch Shopping	0.2
14	Writing Focus	0.1
15		
16		
17		
18		
19		
20		
21		
22		
23		
24		

A few key examples of my interpretations of difficulty:

» Reducing Reddit, Facebook, etc: I knew there were tools online that made it very easy to limit my usage without having to exert any willpower—thus they are ranked very easy.

» Cutting snooze: "easy!?" you ask. Sure. Break the snooze button (what I did) on your clock or put it on the other side of the room. When you know you *can't* snooze, you'll get up.

» Reducing email: a bit harder because it will require time investment to clear in the inbox and unsubscribe to a bunch of stuff (both MIT lists and other mail).

» Improving reading and writing is actually probably the hardest of the group. Not strictly speaking *hard*, and I went after it later, but I got the *really* easy stuff first.

I could meet my 3.2 hour goal with **only the top four** of my Time Recovery Projects (isn't the 80/20 rule a beautiful thing?). I went for six in my queue (not all at once) to be safe in case some of the projects didn't work out.

C)   Executing Time Recovery Projects

Tools: You gotta pick these yourself, buddy

Now that we know which projects to go after, we need to pick the right tools. Most of these are habits and we discuss habitualization in further detail in Part III, "Staying On Track and Focused."

At the end of the day, you're going to have to find or develop your own solutions. I'll provide some examples to inspire you, but I can't give you the answer that will work for you best. It'll take some work from you.

In short, now that we understand the projects we can take on that will make big changes most easily, we're going to make them. A little bit of work, a huge difference.

Execution: Step by Step

For your top-priority Time Recovery Projects:

1. **Figure out how many you need to tackle to reach your goal**. It shouldn't be many. For now, only focus on these.

2. Figure out for yourself **how many at a time** you can successfully execute. Trust your gut. If you're not sure, do fewer for now, make sure the results are *awesome*, and then iterate.

3. **Understand *why* you have the current behavior**. Is it procrastination, avoidance, or distraction? Do you need a new skill? Are you doing something you could automate?

4. **Determine a lower-time alternative**. That is, whatever you're doing, figure out what else you should be doing instead to get that time back. This may require research or getting help. It will change by the type of project:

   a) **Write explicitly and in detail** any new behaviors or habits you will adopt. If you don't have it spelled out, it's much harder to make it stick.

   b) Purchase and **implement any specific tools or structures** that will help, particularly for automation. Buy the right audiobooks, set up folders and filtering in your mail, add website blockers, configure bill auto-pay, buy a larger laundry hamper. Whatever you need to do.

   c) **Shamelessly seek help** to quickly learn any necessary skills. Search the internet about how to read faster if you have a lot of reading (seriously). Get a good book that teaches the skills you want (but only read the relevant parts!). Get help from a professor or a friend.

5. **Make it stick!** New habits aren't easy. You'll need your own solution, but the below may prompt the right thinking or generally be a guide:

   a) **Rules:** Rather than "be on Facebook less," instead limit yourself to "30 minutes per day." Don't "eat less," instead "no eating X, Y, Z." Write these rules down. Put them on your mirror. Know them and love them… and don't have too many.

   b) **Schedule:** Schedule in when you're allowed to do certain things (Facebook, email, etc). Knowing when you're free means there's light at the end of the tunnel and the temptation is less pressing. My favorite example is having a "cheat day" on my diet (a la <u>The 4-Hour Body</u>). This makes it a lot easier to say no to cookies on Wednesday. Similarly, "work out twice per week" is harder than "work out on Tuesdays and Thursdays." That way there's no fooling oneself that we'll just skip today do it tomorrow.

   c) **Temptation Displacement:** Move the distraction further or make it harder. Or eliminate it entirely. Some of my favorites here are having literally broken the snooze on my alarm clock (now I use an alarm app without snooze[12]); using the LeechBlock[13] Firefox add-on to limit myself to 30 minutes total of social media, Reddit, news, and comics/day (I haven't missed them); and closing the Gmail tab so I don't see the bold **(1)** pop up when I get new mail.

   d) **Configure Gear:** Get creative. For work you want to do in otherwise "dead time," configure your cell phone, laptop, etc to make that work quickly available. Get a mobile RSS reader for the train if you're not ambitious; get audiobooks if you are. Print the paper you need to proofread for reading in line or during plane takeoff.

   e) **Tracking:** Track whether you're complying. We'll get more into this in Part III.

   f) **Motivation:** Stay motivated by raising the stakes. Again, more in Part III

6. **Measure and validate.** Measure your time on the improved task and make sure you met your target. If you don't, you won't know whether something's working or not, and you might be putting in a lot of effort for nothing. Knowing whether it's working will let you know whether to hunker down, tweak, or abandon ship.

7. **Iterate.** When you've successfully locked in the changes, move to the next priorities.

---

12   http://wakenshakeapp.com/
13   https://addons.mozilla.org/de/firefox/addon/leechblock/

Some Other Ideas for Executing Time Recovery Projects for Common Challenges

I generally have a strong aversion to telling you what habits you should and shouldn't have, and I don't like giving lists of tips to adopt *en masse*. The list below is designed to provoke thinking, not substitute for it. But if you're stuck, consider some of the solutions to various projects below. Just make sure to always do what works for you.

» **Writing Papers**: I write quite quickly (even though I do not *type* quickly), so I'll share my process:

- **Pick a thesis early**: decide what you're going to say (and what stance you're going to take—remember, you're writing a university paper, not running for President, so you don't need to agonize over having the perfect stance) with your paper as early as you can. You can *tailor* your reading, note-taking, and thinking to support this thesis and have the concepts largely done by the time you're done reading.

- **Write your outline as you go**: Instead of taking notes and then translating to an outline, I take my notes in a word processor in the form of an outline. I add citations (often with quotes) as I go, even if I don't know where they'll be—I can just copy and paste them. Similarly I write my bibliography as I go.

- **Chop-chop when you're done reading the basics**: Kill the arguments that won't help your thesis you best as soon as you can, and thus you can kill extra reading. *Too much reading* for a research paper is the biggest time-killer I know of.

- **Write from the outline**: Your outline should be your paper—in essence, your paper should be done before you start writing the actual sentences. Spend the time to massage your outline into a structured bullet list that you can read through and get the key point. While it's tempting to just turn this in, you can literally highlight each bullet point and write what you need to in order to elaborate.

  Don't worry if it looks sloppy at first—when you go back and read it again, you can change it quickly.

- **Longer ain't better**: You might have page minimums, but beyond that, longer ain't better. In fact, a good professor knows that if you can make your point more briefly, it's more effective. More citations aren't better, either—

most students think professors will love a hundred citations that they scraped around for. Professors aren't stupid and they'll know either that you "just found some" to look impressive or that you spent way too much time reading and not enough time making a point.

- **Remember what's important:** When you read through your paper, focus more on whether you have *sound arguments* that are clear, and less on whether your grammar is perfect… unless, of course, it's a grammar class. 80/20, guys.

- **Use Evernote:** Take pictures of your notes and get 'em on Evernote. They're amazingly easy to search through and this makes life a whole lot easier when getting to citations. I didn't do this in college but it's a fabulous tool.

» **Problem Sets:** The biggest key here is <u>80/20</u>. I look at every problem set as an opportunity to *learn*, rather than *achieve perfection*. If I've learned what I need to learn from a problem, I'm happy—typically the bulk of your grade is from tests. I don't go for the last 20%, typically, as it involves lots of refining and often finding little math errors that have nothing to do with learning the topic. What I *do* is show my work and often draw arrows with "step 1… 2…" etc in order to show my TA how to follow my work. You'll get hosed if people don't know your thinking—and showing your thinking is the best way to make a TA happy and help them understand enough to give you as much partial credit as possible.

Contrary to me, I know people that make their P-Sets *perfect*, re-write them at least once (or type them out with pretty fonts and formatting) staying up all night to do so. It's crazy. Look at it this way: if you only get 70% on your P-Sets (in a standard grading scheme) and they're worth 10% of your grade, that only knocks three points off your final grade, and you can focus more time on nailing your tests, where it matters.

» **Reading:** <u>Don't</u>. <u>Read</u>. <u>Everything</u>. Remember you're a grown-up now and your job is to *learn* (and demonstrate that you learned), not blindly follow a list of instructions. In grad school classes (in the social sciences, like mine), you might have three classes that each assign you a book per week to read and understand. And they're big books. They don't expect you to read every word, they expect you to understand it[14]. Honest professors will tell you themselves that many books could be articles, but you can't sell articles. Here are a few specific techniques:

- **Read the table of contents first:** this often spells out the key points. Select what you'll read and what you'll skim.

---

14   There are exceptions here and you can be honest in asking your TAs—they'll typically give it to you straight. If you're a Philosophy major you probably need to pay very close attention.

- **Find the article the book's based on**: read that first—many parts of the book will be an elaboration on this.

- **Hunt down the thesis and key points**: this applies to both liberal arts and science books. At the end of the day, everyone is saying, "X is true" or "A causes B," followed by "here's why that's true." Make sure you know what those are and understand what the supporting evidence is (and where it could be flawed so you can challenge or discuss it).

- **Skip the parts not meant for you**: depending on the kind of article or book you're reading, some material is meant for audiences that aren't you. If you're a biology major, you don't need to read the section on gel electrophoresis in "methods." If you're a civil engineering major, don't read the part about acquiring zoning permits in your book about building bridges.

- **In any academic paper, if you get what's going on within the first two sentences in a paragraph, skip to the last sentence**. Almost guaranteed the rest is elaboration. Try it.

» **Research**: Start with Wikipedia. Every. Time. It'll give you the gist of what's going on and might point you to some really good more primary reading (might not). Move on to secondary sources before going to primary sources. This way you should be able to find a *few bits of very specific* primary sources you need to read for clarification or validation.

» **Lab Work**: Learning a new machine in the lab (especially if you'll be using it repeatedly) or doing a new process? Look it up on the internet—someone's simplified it. There's probably even a good step-by-step out there on YouTube. Be obsessive about experimental design and get 80% of your help and feedback on that—if you screw that up, you're doing your experiment again.

» **Engineering**: If you're designing a project, look at a few projects that have been designed before. Find common elements and think about why they might be there (you might want to *challenge* those rather than copy them).

» **Programming**: Often someone's written the library you're about to build. There are incredible amounts of open-source stuff out there. If you're trying to *learn* how to do these things, don't scrape code and miss the learning, that's dumb. If it's not critical to learn it (or you already know what you need to know), try not to waste your time writing it and then hunting down bugs.

» **Languages**: Bending over flashcards for hours on end is a waste of those hours. For each new vocabulary word you're trying to memorize, use mnemonics explicitly[15] (I even drew pictures on my flashcards) rather than simply trying to map the translation. Additionally, use the proven Pimsleur method[16] to space out recall practice over increasingly long intervals—this not only saves you time but also significantly improves recall versus a giant block of memorizing.

Hopefully this gets the idea across. "Better focus" in general will also make a huge difference in how much time it takes to do anything—more on this in Part IV.

Example 2: Erik's Six Weekly Time Recovery Projects

Remember I wanted to get at least 3.2 hours back from six projects. Over two weeks I implemented all of these to good effect. Here's how I did it:

Project	Reduce Reddit	Read over Meals	Reduce Facebook	Reduce Email	Walk w/ Audiobook	Cut Snooze
Reason(s)	Temptation; used as procrastination	Tough to use on phone, initially	Temptation; used as procrastination	Too much email! Check frequently as procrastination	Hadn't thought of it yet, need audiobooks	Too tempting for sleepy Erik
Solutions	• New rule: 20 mins of reddit in 1 chunk/day • Scheduled as break between work blocks rather than own time • Unsub 80% of subreddits	• Added RSS feed reader app to phone • Axe bookmarks on laptop • Added only top blogs, comics, news, etc	• Stop auto-login • Axe all email notifications • Eliminate all but most important FB notifications • Schedule in FB checking 2x/week (turns out I didn't miss it at all)	• Search archives for mail for mass unsubscription • Filter out lower-priority mail (dorm spam, events, etc) • 2x scheduled 20-min blocks • Answer most emails in bullets	• Found audiobooks for social science/ humanities classes • Loaded into iPhone	• Broke the snooze button on my clock • Got a clock app *without* snooze!
Making it Stick	• Track w/ RescueTime • LeechBlock	• Track w/ RescueTime • LeechBlock	• Track w/ RescueTime • LeechBlock	• Track w/ RescueTime • Eliminate Gmail from startup tabs	• Unload music for 1 week to habitualize using audiobook	• Sticks on its own ☺

It took a few weeks, and I had relapses, but stuck to it. To help, I had a strict, clear schedule and a set of rules taped to my window to remind me. Along with using the schedule I **got back over four hours per day (average) within two weeks**[17].

So, there you go. Get to it!

---

15   For a bit on mnemonics, see here: http://remembereverything.org/keyword-method/
16   http://en.wikipedia.org/wiki/Pimsleur_method
17   After this, of course, I went much further into spending less time on my given academic workload.

PART II
BRILLIANT EXECUTION EVERY DAY

Up until now, we've been planning: planning our college semesters, our major projects, our months and weeks; even planning Time Recovery Projects. While a great plan is the most important part of getting done what you want to, knowing how to execute effectively is close behind. As the Germans learned the hard way in the 20th century, no plan survives contact with the enemy (in our case, this "enemy" to our plans is reality). This means you need to be attentive, prepared, flexible, determined, and focused. (We'll get more into focus and motivation in Part III)

Here, we'll introduce a system for daily execution, and then a few rules for how to not blow it.

CHAPTER 6 DAILY EXECUTION: THE SYSTEM

I'm going to present below a bare-bones, simple system that requires a minimum of tools and overhead. The principles particularly important here are **remaining results-focused** and *not* **doing work that's not the most important.**

Write every daily task in terms of results. Whether in your work block on your calendar or in a to-do list (below), describe what you'll get done. "Working on something" for two hours is strictly meaningless. A target of how many pages you read is slightly better, but (for instance) "understand Green's Theorem" is a lot better. The reasons for this are simple: first, if your top priority for the day isn't getting done in the estimated amount of time, you still need to do it. Alternatively, if you do get the result in less than the estimated time, you'll know what time you have free. Finally, this clarity simply makes sure we're not wasting our time and are challenging ourselves as to whether what we're doing will best promote our goals. A few examples:

» Bad: "Read German." Better: "Finish Chapter 2 in German." Best: "Know the vocabulary for Quiz 2 on Monday"

» Bad: "Two hours in lab." Better: "Complete the magnetic experiment." Best: "Collect data to prove magnetic force is fully conservative within $p < 0.05$"

» Bad: "Work out for two hours." Better: Run 10k and finish lifting routine."

At some point this results-based detail will become *implied* in your mind… don't let the writing-it-down process become overly bureaucratic.

Love the calendar. As we discussed in "Crush Each Week," the calendar keeps us on task and also helps increase our confidence that everything will be done in its due time so that we don't let other priorities distract us when we're working on one. It's not enough to know what needs to get done during the day—having the day scheduled means nothing falls through the cracks or sneaks up on us at the end. Schedule in free time and social time so work doesn't creep into fun and fun doesn't creep into work.

Review and edit the plan in the morning. You've hopefully scheduled much of your calendar during your weekly planning cycle, but take a look at it every day and edit as necessary—new information will have emerged on Thursday that you didn't have on Monday. I like to print mine out and keep it in my notebook, though this is not for everyone.

Know when it becomes unnecessarily bureaucratic. You'll eventually reach a point where certain blocks of time will be so repetitive or their work so clearly implied that spending time over-clarifying the calendar may not be necessary.

Put unscheduled priorities on a to-do list. We don't know everything we need to do ahead-of-time, even in the morning. Additionally, some tasks are small and don't need their own "block." Here's how we deal with them:

> » **What belongs in these to-do lists** are any tasks that are short (less than half an hour) and timing-agnostic (answering emails or writing a postcard). If it's on your to-do list and either long or time-dependent, get it in your calendar as a block.

> » **The priority system of urgency and importance.** I suspect you've seen the 2x2 grid before of "urgency" and "importance," but if not, I've outlined it below. It describes how you should prioritize different tasks on your to-do list. Obviously high urgency and high importance tasks go first, but it's a generally accepted rule that if it's high importance and low urgency, it comes before its reverse counterpart. Obviously this all exists on a continuous scale, but use it to put a priority to every task, and when you work on your to-do list you'll go after them in that order.

	Low Urgency	High Urgency
High Importance	Priority 2	Priority 1
Low Importance	Priority 4	Priority 3

Here's a sample to-do list that I actually used on August 6th. It was drawn up in the morning and you'll note some of it is "big" enough that it really needs to move into the calendar. The numbers in circles are priorities.

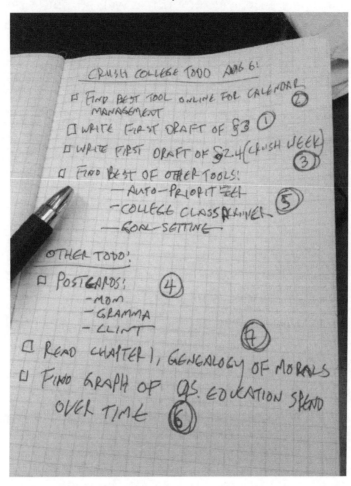

Your inbox as your to-do list (optional): When I'm in environments where I have continuous Internet (I wasn't when the above to-do list was written), I usually use my email inbox as a to-do list. There are a number of advantages to this:

» If someone wants me to do something, they almost always email me, so it's already there, and I can reply + archive to clear it from the list

» I can add something to the list anywhere by emailing myself from my phone. I typically put "H," "M," or "L," in the title to determine where I think it's going to end up on the priority list. This isn't perfect because priorities are ultimately relative, but it's often approximately right

» It's always accessible as my phone's always in my pocket

> » When it gets long, it's scary as hell and makes me take action

It's ultimately a personal choice here, but I really value the technique. It requires clearing your inbox pretty thoroughly—archiving as much as you can, putting lots of mail into folders, et cetera. For me, if my inbox gets longer than five emails, I get distressed and deal with it (usually by taking a little bit of otherwise "free" time to hammer it out).

Add time for the to-do list to your calendar. Create a block in your calendar just called "to-do list" to deal with all this stuff in one fell swoop. You'll find that after a few weeks you won't need a whole lot of time, and if I finish my to-do list early I get to goof off a bit.

Re-prioritize as new information comes up. New information will emerge. Tasks will be thrown at you from your professors, club members, and other peers. You'll make a break-through in the lab that changes your approach to your research project. In short, conditions will change. When they do, take some time to quickly re-prioritize.

> » **On the schedule.** If you find yourself pulled into a meeting, or if a friend comes to you for help and you spend a few hours with them, that's fine: just move your calendar around. Since something new showed up, you won't do everything you originally planned to do. This may mean less free time, it may mean some work gets pushed off 'till tomorrow. Just move the displaced stuff into the calendar block for the lowest-priority thing for the day, unless it already *was* the lowest-priority thing, at which point you can either move it back or not do it (see the Rules for "triage").

> » **On the to-do list.** This one's easier. If a new priority emerges, just re-write the numbers. If I need to squeeze something in, I may write a fraction (like "2.5") to avoid having to re-write all the other numbers.

Be flexible given your situation. If your situation—or environment—changes, what you work on may change. If you find yourself away from a computer, or if your Internet cuts out, you may need to find the highest-priority thing that *fits* the situation at hand. So, if you lose Internet, you won't be checking your email, but you can still write a paper. If you forgot your laptop, you're going to be reading or some such task. Just check your calendar and to-do list when you find yourself in an unexpected situation and work on the highest-priority thing that you can.

Master the art of micro-efficiency! Luckily, being situationally aware doesn't just mean staying on your game when your situation makes your life harder… it also means taking advantage of time that may not have been scheduled for work to get something done. Turn what would otherwise be dead time into time to get something done so you can have more quality free time later. Let's look at a few examples:

- » **Plane takeoff**. Lots of people play Angry Birds during boarding, and when they have to put it away they turn to the in-flight magazine, the lowest form of human publication on the planet. What a waste! Bring a book you need to read or do your planning for how you'll use your in-flight time, what you'll do when you land, et cetera.

- » **Public transit**. Sometimes you can sit, sometimes not. If you can sit, pop out the ol' laptop and get to work. Otherwise, read. If you can't sit, you've hopefully got your audiobook ready at the helm and you can listen.

- » **Standing in line or waiting for a friend**. Pull out your phone and check email or your RSS feed (rather than Facebook). Archive what you can as quickly as you can so the inbox is shorter later. Then move on to short-answer or read-only emails.

- » **Bring stuff out and in with you**. Whenever you leave the dorm, think briefly about whether you should bring laundry or trash out, or bring food in from the store, rather than these trips adding new transit time.

- » **Double-up in the shower**. I love a 20-minute cold shower every morning[1]. I brush my teeth, floss, and shave during this time and none of it is wasted just standing there (though "just standing there" may be your thing—in which case don't let me take that away!). I have my cake and eat it, too.

- » **Briefly consider order-of-operations**. Anyone experienced in cooking has this instinct developed. Always pre-heat the bloody stove first-thing. Marinade or thaw stuff overnight. Cook meals that use both the oven and the stove so you can cook both at once. Wash dishes while the onions sauté. Taking one or two minutes to consider order of operations (remember SMED from "Ruthlessly Eliminating Waste?" you can quickly do this in about a minute) saves gobs of time.

You get the idea. Ultimately, micro-efficiency is less a matter of prescription and more a matter of awareness, attitude, and preparation. If you're bent on eliminating dead time, prepared for any situation, and thinking on your feet, you can almost always be doing something of value. If it's too stressful, don't worry; but challenge yourself about what will make you more accomplished, more satisfied, and (most importantly) less burdened later—thus more free.

Preparing for upcoming situations. To elaborate on the "preparation" section of micro-efficiency, I want you to take 10 minutes *right now* and evaluate your gear—it'll pay off within a day. Here's how to be prepared, step by step:

---

1   Don't knock it 'till you try it, bro.

» **Consider what you always carry.** This should include a smartphone at minimum. I usually carry a backpack and this makes life easy, but you might not, meaning you shouldn't necessarily prepare for being able to work on a laptop. Ladies, if you carry a big purse, you might be able to fit a tablet if you have one.

» **Consider what you do during the week that can be done with what you carry.** Smartphones are great, as you can do almost anything: read the news or a book, listen to an audiobook, check email, do your banking, or check your Facebook if you must. If you carry a backpack, you can put a few slim items in there such as a laptop, tablet, or paperback.

» **Match these tasks to different dead-time environments.** There will be times when you can sit and work (train), times where you can't access Internet (subway), times where you have to stand (in line), and times where you can only listen (walking). Each is more limiting than the previous, but if you're prepared for all of them, you don't have to suffer dead-time.

CHAPTER 7 THE RULES OF DAILY EXECUTION: BREAK THEM AT YOUR OWN RISK

We discussed earlier that no plan survives contact with the enemy. "The enemy" is tumult, distraction, schedule changes, new tasks thrown at you, et cetera. Here we outline a few rules that will *harden you* against this enemy, and will help you respond when the enemy is irresistible and victorious. Frequent interruptions and changes are why many people throw up their hands and don't even bother planning; I think this is an excuse that can and *must* be overcome. Quit thinking of yourself as a victim of fate and take control.

Saying "no" to new work. This is a "hardening" tactic, but for many people, it's a psychologically difficult one. My former boss (who is brilliant and responsible for many of my own idioms) said that "this word, 'no,' is the toughest and most important word to add to one's professional vocabulary." It's important for your college vocabulary, too: it limits the amount of unnecessary work that you have to do that gets put upon you by others. I'm not saying "never help anyone," but I am saying, "don't be a pushover" and don't do work that is someone else's responsibility.

That said, if it's important to someone you care about, will help a meaningful relationship, or if it's part of an obligation that you've taken on, don't dodge it. It's not classy and it's not helpful for you. Don't be that guy: nobody likes that guy. I'm very happy to help my friends and people I care about and will go to the ends of the earth for them. I don't want to help you to become a selfless, empty jerk; I want to help you not do work that it doesn't make sense for you to do.

When you should say "no:" the world will, over and over, ask you to do work that is not your responsibility. This plague befalls the competent with the most frequency. However, you can say "no" to peers, professors, admins, and others. The principles for saying no are as follows:

» **If it's someone else's responsibility, you shouldn't do it**. People may try to offload their work onto you, especially if you're in a club together or in a group in class. Don't do it. You can *help them* with a key part they're stuck on—often they are looking to you to do it because it's difficult for them and easier for you.

» **If you can't see how it will help you more than your other priorities, don't do it.** "Winning brownie points" is a very legitimate benefit *in the right contexts*, but most people vastly over-estimate the value. When someone's asking you for something, think about whether they're someone whose gratitude you really want, and whether that gratitude will turn into a better relationship or just more requests for you to do their work. There are some obvious instances in which you get no benefit out of external work: a survey for the school newspaper is an example. Some are less obvious: as a grad student, I resisted taking on extra work for professors where a strong relationship wasn't really important to me. Besides the few professors that stood out from the crowd, most have very short memories and simply expect that grad students will do their bidding. You won't get many brownie points from many professors, and many will never return the favor for your efforts. In short: choose your brownie points very carefully.

How to say "no": It's scary to tell someone you won't do something! We're constantly afraid of others becoming offended. When I got into consulting I became horrified at the idea of telling a client I couldn't or wouldn't do something for them. Let's discuss the ways we can do this without sounding like a total jerk:

» **Pushing back:** I realized at some point that if someone asks me, "do you have ten minutes," there is *not* a yes/no answer. The answer is always, "it depends what you're proposing I do with those ten minutes." I never have ten minutes for someone to sell me a new insurance plan—I always have ten minutes if my friends are in need, no matter what my situation.

  • Given this reality, you can honestly tell people, "**I don't have the time for this.**" You're in college and people understand you're busy, and if what's being proposed isn't important to you, then no—you don't have time.

  • If you need to clarify that **something is someone else's obligation**, do that. Just as you wouldn't want to pressure Joe into doing Mary's work by mistake, other people don't want to do that to you, either.

  • Finally, you can clarify that **it may not be best for you to do something instead of the person asking**. This is common as a manager, in which direct reports will often learn much more by making a first attempt at something before getting your help. This is the hardest for me as I love helping my team and my instinct is not to send them away, but they grow faster by doing the work themselves. (TA's should pay particular attention here.)

» **Not responding**: If I get an email that says I need to do something in the next hour, it's not going to happen. Part of this is because I just don't check my email more than twice per day. For requests like this, the person asking has a false sense of urgency: if it *really* needed to be done in the next hour, you'd have gotten a phone call or a text. Mass emails will also rarely get a response from me: if the sender thinks it's important that everyone emailed do something, they'll email a specific group.

» **Not doing more work than you need to**. Often people ask you to do something because they know you're good at it, and they're struggling with it. If someone wants your help in this way, define for them the way you're willing to help them in which you add the value of your skill without taking on the work that they can just as easily do. An example: if someone wants my help finding a job, I'll ask them to search through my LinkedIn contacts, email me who they want me to reach out to, add a resume and cover letter for each, and *then* I'll (very happily!) contact my connections and add my own glowing commentary. It means zero unnecessary work for me *and* it gets the person asking a better result in the end. Nobody is going to be resentful that I didn't spend two hours on LinkedIn looking at my *own* contacts and trying to guess who might be a good match.

How to avoid having to say "no". Even for me, telling people I won't do something they want to do sucks. There are good ways to avoid the influx of requests for you to do something—often, problems get solved on their own when people can't toss them over the fence into your yard.

» **Make yourself scarce**. I'm rarely on chat[1]. When I'm on chat, not only am I distracted, but it's easy for people to bother me. With *higher* barriers to putting work on me, people will tend to ask me to do more important work, rather than less important stuff that ends up solving itself without my intervention.

» **Build a reputation**. I have a powerful reputation among my friends for helping them without reservation when it's important… and a reputation for being honest about limiting my engagement where it doesn't make sense to be there. By having this reputation, I tend to only get requests where it really makes sense for me to help. This way, I can devote more time to where I really make a difference. An example here: after a nightmare three-hour ride home one day dropping off

1   When I am on chat, I'm labeled as "busy" and only talking to the folks I want to talk to.

three colleagues at three different locations, I created a rule in which I would drop colleagues off at subway or bus stations within a limited radius from my route or house. As the only one in the group paying insurance and maintenance (they're great about splitting gas), I've chosen to not *also* bear the burden of chauffeuring everyone to their doors and being the last person home every day.

When to triage: This former boss of mine is also responsible for the quote, "prioritization is about what you *won't* do." We do have limited time and therefore we'll only do so many things. If break-in work has to happen today or if a high priority takes longer than expected, I quickly select what I *won't* do at all. This may mean eating a salad (quick to make) rather than the elaborate dinner I was planning. It might mean not writing a blog post I was planning on. It might mean no Facebook at all. If the break-in "work" was social time, maybe I won't *also* have a big social time block in the future at the detriment of work (I might show up later to a party). The point here is to find the lowest-priority stuff and, if possible, triage it.

When to re-schedule: If *nothing* in your day can go away completely (there are days like this!), you need to reschedule your time and triage something later down the line so you can get the lower priorities into the schedule. You may have a bunch of "unscheduled" time in the future and you can put the work there… but it means that time won't be used for something else. Such is reality.

Our process makes us much more aware of any wasted time in our lives than we used to be. If something takes longer than expected or if break-in work comes in, it's easy to fall into the trap of lamenting the lost time and getting bent out of shape about it. We need to accept that we'll never be perfect, and that this is totally fine—you're directing much more if your time to what's important to you than you ever have before, and this should be only celebrated.

The Final Word

The world is constantly messing with your plan, and this is okay. Sometimes, new high priorities come in, and we need to reprioritize on the fly and cut out the lowest priority we have. Be cool and flexible: the fact that you have a plan means you can change it without panicking. When work comes our way that *isn't* a priority, we need to say no. It's one of the hardest things to do in the world. Just remember that being a wonderful, helpful person isn't about dropping everything to do everyone else's work, or about sacrificing your own well-being to make their lives a little more convenient. By all means, be a pillar of support, and take great pride in doing this! But there's no sense in taking on work when you don't add any real unique value to someone's life: save your limited capacity to help others to when you really change the game—or when they really need the support. Even if you put less *time* into supporting others than you used to, you're going to be much more helpful (and beloved) for it.

PART III
STAYING ON TRACK AND FOCUSED

This is the part that most people (at any age, of any profession) know they could improve dramatically. All of us succumb to distraction—it's natural. But man, is it a time-killer. Like other aspects of crushing college, most people that struggle with this think they're missing some core virtue, that "being better," "working harder," and generally feeling bad about oneself are the keys to improvement. Others don't believe improvement is possible. When you see those with focus superpowers, remember: they have a process for keeping their brains in "focus mode." The process will differ for different people, but there's nothing at all stopping you from developing your own.

This Part will be short. There's a whole lot of material on this topic; this is where most "productivity" books focus exclusively. I will be summarizing the best of it, adding my own limited commentary, and pointing you to the source for concepts you want to explore further.

We'll cover two separate concepts in the following chapters, both of which are important:

Staying on Track: *this is all about making sure behavioral changes and new habits stick. If you're trying to lose weight, go on Facebook less often, etc, this chapter covers that.*

Staying Focused: *even if we have Facebook locked away, it can be hard to focus. We might get distracted by every person walking by or just stare at our paper until our eyes melt, getting nothing done. This chapter covers how to turn your work time into high-octane results by staying focused and hammering out really good work.*

CHAPTER 8 STAYING ON TRACK: ADOPTING NEW HABITS AND MAKING THEM STICK

Habits ain't easy to change. You know it, I know it, researchers know it. Unfortunately, most folks trying to change a habit use self-deprecation, guilt, and shame to improve their performance, when all evidence suggests that these behaviors *detract* from your ability to change your behaviors.

To better understand *how* to improve our ability to adopt new habits, we need to understand our own brains a bit better. Doing this means we can manipulate our subconscious and use our own natural tendencies—which often seem to be the source of our worst habits—and turn them to our advantage.

A.   Our Brains: Willpower and Habit

There are a number of excellent models or analogies that describe how our brains operate. I'll share a few, and then the key takeaways:

Switch: **The Elephant, the Rider, and the Path**. In Switch, Chip Heath describes our psyche as split between the Elephant and the Rider. The Elephant is your impulsive, emotional self; the Rider is your rational self with foresight and plans. The Rider sits upon the Elephant and tries to direct him along the Path to a goal. But, of course, the Elephant tends to be easily distracted by temptations along the way, and has little desire to push through particularly tough obstacles.

Most people try to keep the Elephant on track by yanking harder at the reins, kicking it, etc. As you already know from experience, your "Elephant" tends not to respond well to this. To successfully get the Elephant to go where you want, the clever Rider takes time to shape the Path by lessening the obstacles, removing temptations that take the Elephant off the Path, and by placing temptations on the Path to keep the Elephant marching with vigor.

The Willpower Instinct: Our Two Brains. In <u>The Willpower Instinct</u>, Kelly McGonagall describes that the brain is quite literally divided into two parts. The impulsive, instinctual brain evolved before *homo sapiens* and drives us through urges, instincts, habits, and emotions. It gives us hunger, excitement, shame, and exhaustion. At the end of the day, it is both helpful and absolutely necessary to our survival and happiness, but it's not always the appropriate half of the brain to use in the modern first world (which notably lacks saber-toothed tigers, famine, or rival tribes).

The other half of the brain is the pre-frontal cortex, capable of planning, rational thought, and the ability to "say no:" to act against our instinctual brain's urges when we know it's not appropriate. It is also powerful, but its ability to veto the instinctual brain (called "willpower") can be exhausted, like a muscle. And, like a muscle, we can both strengthen our willpower it over time and also reduce the "force" and frequency necessary in applying it to stick to what we want.

McGonagall also points out that research shows that those who "beat themselves up" or make themselves feel guilty when they fail a willpower challenge are *more likely* to fail again, and sooner (I liken it to "beating the Elephant when it goes off the Path"), which is critically important to remember going forward.

My commentary on the key takeaways from reading these: There are a few principles we should understand about the brain that will make a major difference in our efforts to stick to changing our habits:

» **Our brains aren't 100% rational.** The "Elephant," or instinctual brain, is an undeniable, powerful, and important part of who we are. It is going to exert force on us and pretending that it doesn't exist is going to lead to failure.

» **"Just trying harder" doesn't work.** The Rider does indeed succeed in keeping the Elephant on path hundreds or thousands of times per day, and we often don't even notice. But in those places where you repeatedly fail to keep yourself on track, you have a situation where your Elephant is currently more powerful than your Rider. You will *have to make changes* in your Path or go through exercises to improve your willpower in order to succeed in these.

» **Guilt backfires.** Now that you understand your brain a bit better, you should be more able to forgive yourself—you're not a weak or bad person if your instinctual "Elephant" brain wins; you just need to change the Path. Feeling bad about it ("kicking the Elephant") provably only makes you more likely to seek out comfort, which is typically in the form of whatever habit you're trying to kick (eating, Internet, et cetera). Self-forgiveness and dispassion are critical. What does "dispassion" mean? It means looking at a willpower failure and analytically asking "how did the system break down? How can I improve it?" I can't stress this enough—not only will it work better than the old "guilt" model, but your life will become a whole lot less stressful[1].

» **You can adopt habits that overall increase your willpower**. Think of it as tipping the balance in favor of the rational pre-frontal cortex. We'll discuss techniques in the following pages, but some of them are as simple as "working out" and "getting sleep."

» **You can turn your Elephant from enemy to friend**. By moving the Elephant's temptations onto the Path, your Elephant charges ahead without your Rider exerting itself (you exerting willpower). This is by far my favorite method, and we'll discuss this in the following pages.

B.   Methods for Improving Willpower and Sticking To Habits[2]

For whatever habit you're going to change, let's discuss briefly what works. There are no guarantees on what's going to be the best model for you, but it seems *any* of the below tend to have a positive impact on sticking to new habits. I can more-or-less guarantee that without implementing any of the below, you're going to struggle or—as so many do—fail in conquering your toughest challenges of habit.

When in particular we're trying to *quit* an old habit (rather than pick up a new one), we are often suffering from a mild mental addiction[3]. Dopamine, the chemical in our brain that says "yes, do this!" and promises reward for it, drives us to our old habits and to distractions like email or Facebook. Dopamine indeed leads us to all our addictions, from shopping to narcotics. Unfortunately, dopamine convinces you to buy things or spend time on a website against your better judgment, so the temptations that pull you in most are often *specifically designed* by companies to press that dopamine button[4]. So I want

---

1   If this doesn't feel obvious to you in a deep, emotional way, read The Willpower Instinct—McGonagall is much more eloquent on this topic than I am. If you're the kind of person who spends much of your time beating yourself up and can't imagine living without that, I urge you to also read Byron Brown's Soul Without Shame in order to silence your inner critic. These books changed my life.

2   These techniques come from a wide array of sources. McGonagall, Heath, Stephen R. Covey, Tim Ferris, and Byron Brown are responsible for most.

3   I know this term is very scary in the United States, but I want us to be very honest with ourselves here.

4   You may know the "dopamine button" experiment for rats in cages in which they kept pounding at the button—it would spike them with dopamine when they did—until they collapsed from exhaustion (or

you to understand that you're going to have to be equally clever to reduce the dopamine cravings for bad habits and *increase* them for good habits. "Fighting" your own brain here seldom works. Let's take a look at some of these clever tactics below.

Improve your willpower—short term. A lot of different mental and physiological states sap willpower just like they sap your physical muscles. Here are the key states to focus on improving:

» **Sleep**! Sleep-deprivation is the willpower-killer. "But I have too much to do to sleep!" I hear you say. Consider the *positive* feedback loop of getting sleep: one gets enough sleep, willpower improves, one gets work done faster and earlier, and has time to sleep. Take time to get caught up (I know this is blasphemy, but maybe you can skip a party or a problem set) and make sure it's a priority.

» **Exercise**: Similarly, an un-exercised body has a whole lot less willpower. Don't have time? You have enough time for the 7-Minute Workout[5]. It's enough time to get the job done (for both cardiovascular health and improved willpower). I like to get to the gym and lift.

» **Mood**: Frustration, sadness, and anxiety hurt willpower. A peaceful disposition improves it. Volumes are written on how to improve one's mood—I personally use bursts of mindfulness meditation[6] (as short as five or ten minutes). If you're frequently angry[7] or moody[8], I have some reading that's helped me, but talking to someone professional may be where you need to go if mood is a persistent problem for you.

» **Food**: Keeping a moderate and steady blood sugar level dramatically improves willpower (also keeps you from falling asleep midday). This means lower glycemic index foods in your diet—dropping lots of the sugars, starches, and other simple carbs.

Improve your willpower—long term. Like a regular muscle, we exercise it! This may not sound fun, but bear with me: according to McGonagall, the best way to do this is to frequently win a *very tiny* willpower challenge. The example she had was about a man trying to stop eating candy. The first thing he did (and only change for a whole month) was to place a jar of jelly beans in the hallway that he walked by frequently. While allowed to eat

---

did even more self-destructive stuff). They're not allowed to do this to rats anymore.

5   http://well.blogs.nytimes.com/2013/05/09/the-scientific-7-minute-workout/%3F_r%3D0

6   Mindfulness Meditation is a practice of focusing quietly on one thing in order to train the mind to focus better—just like a muscle. The most basic form of this practice is closing your eyes and focusing on your breath, feeling it come in and out, and letting go of thoughts in your mind as they enter. Jon Kabat-Zinn's "Mindfulness for Beginners" is the most accessible guide on this.

7   The Anger Trap by Les Carter.

8   Emotional Awareness by the Dalai Lama and Paul Ekman.

any other candy, he said "no" to this jar. Although he didn't commit to anything more in that month, he found himself able to (for the first time) resist the candy jars at his coworkers' desks after a few weeks. The takeaway here is if you want to improve your willpower, create tiny willpower challenges for yourself that are easy to conquer, and be aware of every time you win.

Make the Path simple. In short, simplify and clarify your goals. Poorly defined goals are incredibly hard to maintain, as are complicated ones. If the Rider is confused about where to go, the Elephant doesn't stand a chance in taking him there. A few examples:

> » "Eat less" is terribly unclear. "Eat <1800 calories" is complicated. "Cut out drinks with calories and anything with sugar" is clearer and more simple.

> » "Less social media" is terribly unclear. "No more than 30 minutes of Facebook" is fine. "No Facebook in the office ever" is quite clear and simple.

Make the path less daunting for the Rider. You may remember back in Part II we broke down big projects into chunks. This makes the path much easier because it's in fact a series of short, simple paths rather than a gigantic one. Besides breaking a new behavior into chunks, we can use a few other techniques to reduce intimidation:

> » **Commit to doing something five times.** Those who jog five times are far more likely to stick with it long-term than those who don't make it that far. Don't look at something as necessarily a commitment *forever* right away. Just commit to five repetitions of whatever the behavior is and it'll get easier to continue.

> » **Set a series of goals.** Be able to declare victory along the way! When I was losing weight, I targeted 10 pounds at a time, publically celebrating each time. It's hard to try to drop 40 pounds (which I did), but easy to go for 10.

> » **Schedule breaks from sticking to the new habit.** Think of it as a campsite along the Path. The best example of this I have is a weekly Cheat Day on a diet, meaning the light at the end of the tunnel for cookies, beer, and pizza is never more than a week away. It's been a game-changer in my success.

Remove obstacles from the Path. Some call this "lowering transaction costs" for good behaviors. The idea is to make it much easier to *start* doing the desired behavior—once you start, it's much easier to keep going. A few examples:

> » A friend of mine sleeps in his gym clothes, with his running shoes right next to his bed, so it's easier to go running in the morning.

> » When I was trying to get into the habit of flossing, I just put the box of floss on top of my toothbrush when I was done. This way I had no choice but to run into it, making it impossible to forget.

» Another friend moved his guitar right next to his computer chair. He wanted to practice more, but he tended to go straight for his computer upon getting home. With his guitar between his bedroom door and his computer chair, it was much easier to pick it up and start playing.

Remove temptations that lead away from the Path (or add obstacles between you and them). Here we make it *very hard* to access distractions or other bad behaviors. As they say at Alcoholics Anonymous: "If you don't want to slip, don't go where it's wet." That applies for you, too. If you're trying not to do something, make it far away and *increase the effort required* to go to these temptations. Take advantage of your own laziness by making it difficult to be distracted. A few examples:

» I never keep my Gmail tab open. This way, on a browser, I never see the **(1)** that tells me I have a new message, and so I don't get distracted to go check it. (Similarly, I have unsubscribed from as many email lists as I can manage so when I do check I only have a few. This keeps me from obsessing over email when I'm doing something else.)

» As I've mentioned before, I use a website blocker called LeechBlock to make sure that I can't access Facebook, Reddit, or news after 30 minutes of total time spent on all three—these are my top computer distractions. There are other good blockers out there and, frankly, you should probably put this guide down and go get one for your browser right now.

» A friend of mine keeps cookies and other sweets locked away, and only the roommates have keys. He can get to them… he just has to muster up the effort to go ask. Much harder than going to the pantry, but it means he doesn't have to clear the house entirely.

***Add* temptations to the Path.** The below are my favorite techniques and have been the most effective for me. Making the path tempting means your Elephant charges forward, and your Rider just has to hang on—obstacles seem trite in comparison! These temptations involve both rewards for getting to the goal *and* effective (but not self-judgmental!) punishments for failure, which are motivating for your instinctual self. A few examples below should illustrate the point:

» **Make Progress Visible:** This is basic and you'll fail without it. Measure your progress and visualize it. Trying to cut back on Facebook? Use RescueTime and get a weekly graph emailed to you. Open it and bask in glory or shame depending on how you performed versus your (very clear, remember?) target.

» **Embrace Public Shame (and Triumph):** When I was losing weight, I wasn't sure how I'd do it (what diet I'd use, etc). What I was sure of was that I was going to publicize the heck out of the effort, turning it into a campaign for myself and entertainment for others. I posted a graph on Facebook of my current and and goal weight, with a little dotted line each week to show progress. I promised my friends to post every week, and I did. Let me tell you: knowing you've got a graph-posting coming up is extraordinarily motivating! We *take advantage* of our "Elephant's" need for social approval, and the Elephant does the rest. I did, by the way, make my target, garnering many "Likes" and such (though I fell just short of my later, more ambitious target). Friends would mention "The Graph" when they'd see me and tell me it was inspiring. I loved it.

» **Crank up Peer Pressure:** Even better than just publicizing a target and progress is getting your friends to routinely heckle you—that way we just can't pretend people aren't paying attention. I asked my roommates to heckle me if they ever saw me drinking something with calories[9] (cola, beer, wine). I have a gym buddy to get me to get off my butt and lift—it's much harder to let someone else down than yourself!

» **Add Bets:** These can come in all shapes and sizes. The most powerful is "StickK[10]," in which you put money in escrow and if you fail to meet your goal, it goes to an Anti-Charity (something you hate). My friend, who is trying to write fiction, has a bet in which I hold his money as escrow and will give it to his least-favorite politician's re-election campaign should he fail in his goals. It turns into a gift for himself if he wins.

» **Make it Competitive:** Like the above, competition goes a long way. Maybe you compete with a friend on building the strongest bridge in your civil engineering class. Race a friend in adding strength or chipping away at your 5k time.

» **Build Up for Something Big:** To get me running, I sign up for obstacle-course mud runs (with friends). I just *would not* do it otherwise, but if I have a few fun 5k's coming up, I get out there and stay in shape for them. Want to motivate yourself on your thesis? Set a date by which you'll submit it for publication. Pay to go to a conference in your field and then try to present your work there—it'll make it a lot more exciting to go to lab.

» **Add Rewards Throughout:** There are rewards of glory that we covered above, but we can give ourselves some others, too. I'll let myself play video games when I get done everything I wanted to for the day. It's like putting a big ol' pile of peanuts (or whatever elephants like) just over the hill on the Path.

---

9   Except, of course, on Cheat Day.
10   http://www.stickk.com/. The founder of StickK, Ian Ayres, has a book called <u>Carrots and Sticks</u>, though I have not read it.

There's a lot up there. For each of the behaviors you're trying to change—look to your Time Recovery Projects for what will most likely be the biggest ones—pick from above and implement with ferocity. Refer back to the "Implementation" section of "Ruthlessly Eliminating Wasted Time" to add structure as necessary.

The Final Word

When you want to change a behavior, you need a plan to stick to it. Be explicit about what that plan is. Write it down and then set up your life to make it easiest to stick to the new behavior, whatever it is. I've shared numerous examples of my own—find the ones that are right for you. *Stack the deck*—while you don't want to get bureaucratic, don't rely on your Rider yanking the reins, but instead adopt as many tools that seem reasonable for your toughest challenges. With them, the impossible becomes a breeze. Don't just read through the above and say, "good idea:" pick the right suite of willpower-enhancing tools to each major change you're making *right now* and then go implement them.

Remember to forgive yourself when you stumble—you always will (I do constantly). When you do, analyze the situation dispassionately and then adjust your system to stack the deck in your favor.

Wait! Here's the point in a book where most people declare, "great idea!" and then move on without implementing anything. If you're just reading through now and will go back for step-by-step work later, that's fine. But if you have behaviors you're currently trying to change, stop reading and go write out explicitly what methods you're going to use to make them stick. Start with one or two.

Done? All right, you may proceed.

CHAPTER 9 LASER FOCUS: AVOIDING DISTRAC-TION AND JUST GETTIN' IT DONE

Focus often seems to come and leave at its own whim. While I've never completely mastered the art of focus (I get distracted, too), there are techniques one can use to dramatically improve it.

Some of focus is willpower, and gets better with steady blood sugar, enough sleep, and exercise. But focus is often about being "in the zone," in which the brain is not throwing distractions at us or catching on to others in the environment. We're at one with whatever we're doing and nothing else is in our minds. How do we get there and, more importantly, how do we *stay* there?

Let's talk first about distractions. I know you already know that you should get rid of them, but you haven't. But these are *the* focus-killers. When trying to increase focus, it may not be *enough* to get rid of distractions, but if you don't, nothing else you do will matter. The trouble with distractions is they don't just kill the time in which you're distracted, but they kill time *after that*. Why is this? The brain has a "warm-up" period for getting focused on a single task. *Every time* you get distracted, you have to "warm back up" to focus, which means you're losing time not only during, but after the distraction. This means we need to be ruthless.

It seems a harsh doctrine at first, but consider this: one gets less done by keeping distractions (Facebook, email, text) at his or her side. If, when we need to focus on our *work*, we keep them at bay, then we have more time later, and can happily and guiltlessly indulge. This doctrine of focus is *not* about completely eliminating pleasure or relaxation from your life; it is about not trying to both work and goof off at the same time. Let each have its own time and place.

Ruthlessly annihilate distractions. Your brain is complex enough that it will happily kick itself out of focus; it doesn't need your help on the matter. When you want to focus, you have to eliminate distractions with extreme prejudice. Start by looking back on a working block and writing down everything that distracted you—your current crush, hunger, Facebook, text messages, emails, Facebook, people walking by, Facebook, new music on your Pandora station, Facebook. Whatever it is. Find them and kill them. Is it harsh? No, it's smart: schedule time for all the "external" distractions—I promise they'll be there when you're done working, and you'll enjoy them more. Here are a few examples:

» **Turn your phone off**. Not silent. Not airplane mode. *Off*. Some people can't do this as they're on call for work or are in charge of a nuclear power plant (as is the case at a few universities out there). Unless you're one of them, there are *no calls or texts that cannot be returned after two hours*. Friends maintained wonderful relationships before text messaging, and so can you. You don't need your apps in the lab, while studying, or writing a paper. It may be very, very hard to kick the habit of texting all the time (especially if you're a typical three-hour-per-day user), but use the techniques above. The constant distraction of texts is probably the single worst distraction we have today.

» **Turn off your laptop's wifi when you don't *absolutely* need it**. Same principles to the phone apply. You'll find yourself instinctively (and unconsciously) opening your browser and the "not connected" page will remind you of what you're doing, pushing you back to work.

» **Block distracting websites wholesale (when you need Internet)**. Everything that could possibly waste your time should be blocked. If you really do want to read the news, schedule in when you read the news during the day (and LeechBlock allows you to schedule when certain sites are un-blocked). Block sites after a certain amount of time spent on them.

» **Kill IM when you need internet**. You see where we're going here.

  • **If you need it turned on, be invisible or "busy"** and talk to only the folks you need to.

  • Once again, you should feel free to socially use IM *when it's that time*, not when it's time to work.

» **Find and eliminate other environmental distractions**. I bite my nails and have to keep them well-filed or they'll distract me. A friend of mine is distracted just by other people moving around, so to get work done he gets seats that face the wall, rather than everyone else at the café. Another friend quite literally wears earplugs (especially if he's anywhere there are children). I have to even be careful about the music I play, because I'll muck around with my music player after every darn song (I play good albums or put on Pandora instead). This process requires a lot of self-honesty, but we already know the principles for success. Take a day and learn yourself.

Set up the environment. Now that we've killed distractions, we can *add* to the environment to enhance focus. This will be an area in which different practices are better for different people, but I want to share below some of the practices that have performed well in studies.

» **Music.** Good music not only eliminates distractions but studies show it is actually *stimulating*. The best kinds of music, it seems, have a few shared traits: they don't have lyrics (as lyrics draw focus), they're consistent in mood (not moving from smooth jazz to heavy metal), and they're not very familiar to you. (The last one was a surprise to me!) This points us to getting a good Pandora or Spotify station. I prefer ambient electronic or IDM; my girlfriend goes for classical.

» **Light.** Be somewhere well-lit. Not surprisingly, your body wants to work during the day and sleep at night, so take advantage of this. Sunlight or full-spectrum bulbs are preferable. Whatever you do, don't work in a dark room: as I'm sure you already know, it makes you tired and strains your eyes.

» **Food and caffeine.** Be well-fed, ideally with something with a low glycemic index, so you don't get a blood sugar crash later. It also just so happens that keeping your blood sugar consistently *high* will amp up your focus, so if you're not worried about your waistline you can choose to eat a Skittle every five minutes or so (that's about the frequency you need) when you *really* need to hammer down[1]. Moderate amounts of caffeine, as predicted, significantly increase focus, but be careful: drinking more than 200mg (two cups of coffee) per day or so increases your tolerance (meaning you don't respond as well to it) and makes you completely useless without it. If you do drink coffee, drink it about 20 minutes before starting the work you need to do: the benefits you will get from a cup of coffee will be at their peak from the 20-minute mark through the next hour.

» **Get your work in front of you.** Commit to opening your paper and scrolling to the part you need to work on, to opening the book you need to read and getting your notebook, or to getting into lab. Once you're there, it's easier to work, just like it's easy to run once you're on the track in your gym clothes and on the track.

---

1   I don't do this.

» **Dress for success.** As crazy as it sounds, putting on clothes you associate with work (button-down shirts, or at least a pair of pants) puts our brain in a disposition to work[2]. Contrast this to the PJs we sleep in. If you're going to read or write or do anything productive, get dressed.

» **Get comfy—but not too comfy.** Don't work in your bed. Like your PJs, it tricks part of your brain into thinking it's bedtime. Work in a chair, upright, but be comfortable (lean back rather than hunch and extend your legs a bit), lest aches distract you.

Get in the zone. Here's the hardest part for most people. They sit down and it's an hour later before they're actually working. Once again: as much as you don't want to hear it, you're probably distracted by dopamine-inducing temptations, so killing them is #1. After that, there's a lot we can do to kick your brain into gear:

» **Write down everything you're worried about before working.** This could be a to-do list or something concerning you without a clear answer. Whatever it is, having it on paper lets the brain "let it go" for a while, knowing that it's right there and won't be forgotten. This is also why we schedule our week into blocks, keep to-do lists, and set aside time for them: knowing everything will be taken care of means our worries don't pull us away and our brain can get into focus mode.

» **Choose a tangible result you want to achieve.** "Just working" is demotivating. Choose what you'll accomplish during this focus period and it's easier to power through—in part because you know there's an end in sight, and in part because we're motivated by feeling accomplished.

» **"Eat a (small) frog" first.** Mark Twain said, "eat a frog first thing in the morning and nothing worse will happen to you the rest of the day." While eating a particularly large frog means we probably won't get started, eating a "little" one—that is, doing a small chunk of the hardest or most miserable work—means that the rest will be relatively easy and we'll be able to get moving.

» **Tell yourself that it'll be rewarding.** Most of us have no trouble getting really focused when starting a video game. Studying isn't as fun, of course. But, just as you can actually makes yourself *happier* simply by smiling or wishing someone a great day, you motivate the subconscious part of the brain by telling it that what you're doing is rewarding, which can be as easy as reminding yourself about exactly how it relates to your goals in college[3]. We can call this "motivating self-talk."

---

2   I swore by wearing a full suit to an exam, but I have no scientific evidence for this.
3   If it's not related to your top goals in college... why the heck are you doing it? You should be able to make this link clear, and it will help you power through stuff you don't want to do in the moment.

Stay in the zone. Beyond having the right external environment, there are a few surefire things we can do to increase the likelihood we'll stay focused for a while.

> » **Quit complaining**. Just like self-talk can help motivate, it can *certainly* demotivate. In short, resist complaining or you'll kill your motivation. Turns out, the more we complain, the worst we feel *in general*, so I think this is a great life rule. When you catch your inner voice whining, tell it to zip it. It actually helps.

> » **Take breaks**. Most of the time, our focus goes up, peaks, and then starts to drop. If we just try to power through, it often remains low. The "Pomodoro method" claims that these cycles are most often about 20 minutes, and thus it suggests taking a five-minute break after 20 minutes of work. If this works for you (it doesn't for me), use a timer so you're not constantly checking the clock.

> » **Move between projects**. I try to block out no more than three hours in a row for a single project (some people prefer two). Luckily, in college you've got a pretty diverse plate of work. Even if you need to work on something for (say) six hours, you can usually switch to something else for two hours between three-hour blocks at the bigger task.

> » **If you're on a roll, stay there if you can**. Sometimes we really get a lot of momentum and time flies as we're working. If so, don't force yourself away. If you can stay in lab or with your paper during one of these high-focus spurts, do it. Don't even take a long break until you feel you need it. (This means ignoring some of the advice above when you're really switched on!)

> » **Give yourself a reward upon completion**. If I finish my work early (remember each block should have an associated *result*), I let myself use the rest of that block to goof off. I don't always use it to goof off (if I'm on a roll), but it motivates me to get over some of the bigger hills if I know there's an oasis on the other side.

> » **Take up mindfulness meditation**. Experienced meditators can focus on heinously mundane tasks for superhuman amounts of time compared to the general population. Focus is *also* like a muscle that can be trained. If you want to improve it, mindfulness meditation is one of the best ways to do so. If you're not looking for a religious experience, there's plenty of secular meditation material out there[4].

---

4   I recommend Jon Kabat-Zinn's "Mindfulness for Beginners" audiobook for learning how mindfulness meditation with a strictly secular approach.

The Final Word

If you eliminate both external and mental distractions, you're probably 90% of the way to focus: your brain will have few options but to focus on the task at hand, even if you don't want to do it. Do this and you're going to be light-years ahead of your colleagues. After that, be in tune with your own patterns of focus (what food, time of day, music, et cetera work best for you?), improve them where you can, and change your internal dialogue to improve your motivation. The most productive students don't always prefer schoolwork to video games and beer, but they are able to approach their work maturely and, by seeing how it fits into the big picture (and by not whining), they are able to power through without misery.

PART IV
Closing

CHAPTER 10 CLOSING THOUGHTS

If you're like me, you've probably powered through the guide before putting anything into practice. That's good, as it gives me an opportunity to quickly emphasize a few things.

I don't like most "productivity" guides. Surprising? There are a few reasons, and I think they're all critical differences in the way that Crush College looks at the world:

» **They think more work is better (and thus strive to eliminate non-work).** "Work," as measured in number of hours of studying or pages read, is a *terrible* measure of how well you've spent your day or your week. What are you really trying to accomplish, and does it require all those hours or pages? Rarely is this asked, and it's where a huge amount of time is wasted.

» **They don't spend any time defining "productive."** A typical productivity philosophy assumes you already know what the most important result for you is. But we spend *so much of our day* doing crap that's not important to us—this will happen to you even more in your life after college, if you're not careful. It's not "productive" if it's not furthering major goal for you, and an alternative is *more* productive if it furthers a *higher* goal for you. This is the crux of the philosophy here: if you are accomplishing more of what's most important to you (from med school to great nights out with friends), then you're winning—not simply if you're taking more classes or even simply getting better grades.

» **They don't focus on the challenges *you* face.** Many similar guides simply contain long lists of suggested behaviors. It's tempting to simply copy the habits of successful individuals, but it's lazy and ineffective. Your biggest opportunities to eliminate wasted time *will* be different from others, as will the most effective methods you use to make and stick to the changes.

» **They don't help you to *challenge yourself*.** Covey's <u>7 Habits</u>, for example, is ultimately seven very obvious recommendations that are easy to read, agree with, and then ignore. I know that you already know, for example, that you should be on Facebook less. But what I'm asking you to do is reach into your heart and bring forth the truths about what's important to you, and then compare that to how you're spending your time. It's an exercise that is likely to be a bit terrifying, and this is good. There's no sense feeling guilty, but my hope is that this tells you that there is so much more you can do with your life!

The conviction I want you to walk away with after putting this down (for the first time) is that there is a richer, more exciting, more peaceful, more rewarding life out there that all of us can be living. I want you face-to-face with the realization that your college experience—and your *life*—is short and fleeting. This is not a call to irresponsibility and whimsical hedonism: quite to the contrary, it is a call to bring to light your deepest convictions and desires and to run towards them. It is a call to challenge the path that you've been told you *should* take, to challenge the limits of what others tell you is possible or reasonable. It is, hopefully, an inspiration that helps you to believe that you do not need to choose between "living today" and investing in tomorrow, between experience and ambition, but instead that you can have much more of both than you currently do… and that you absolutely should.

This is a call to make the best of the very precious, miniscule flash of time that you have on this earth. It's a call to be happy.

So: don't let anyone (even me!) tell you that you have to double-major—*or* that it's unwise to do so, if it's what you know you want. You're going to find yourself with a whole lot of time on your hands if you don't have a vision of what to do with it, and there is a risk that it will blindly turn into more work or more goofing off. This is why our *first* exercise is to really understand our goals, and this is one of the reasons why it's the single most important exercise in the guide. As you find your time opening up, move more of it to accelerating your highest goals or bringing on new goals further down the list.

What Will You Do With Your New Time?

So, enterprising College Crusher: what'll it be? Run a marathon? Learn a language and study abroad? Get published? Learn cooking or mixology? Host great parties for your friends? Play more games? Get to med school without bags under your eyes and a shortened life expectancy? Graduate early and save a few thousand bucks of tuition? God forbid: perhaps you might take time to learn more both in and out of your classes than is required for A's on your report card? Build a robot? Paint? Write? Read Socrates?

There's so much out there. Don't be fooled by simple whims or daydreams, but do get excited. Experiment. Run towards whatever you set your sights on. And when you've Crushed College, take these principles forward with you: I guarantee they'll be just as important when you start having to make money and live a satisfying adult life.

Now get to it. An incredible life awaits.

CHAPTER 11 FURTHER READING

There's a lot of great reading I've done in my life that's helped me to become a more productive and, ultimately, much happier person. I've listed it in case you'd like to read it, too.

How to live a great life: Hopefully you've had a bit of good introspection about how you're spending your time, and ended up with a few questions about what it means to live a great life. What can one do besides the typical prescribed path of work-drink-work? How does one fill the void once one has all this free time? How can one make choices in college that get the most out of it? A few of these books should take a crack at it:

» Cal Newport, <u>How to Win at College</u>. This is the definitive guide on how to orient the specific resources and options at college to prepare you for the future (and impress the pants off everyone else).

» Clayton M. Christensen, <u>How Will You Measure Your Life</u>? Similarly practical to Newport's book, this is directed at adults and focuses in part on how to build strategies to prepare for future accomplishment in work, family, and personal life—even when we don't yet know what we most want to do in the future.

» Seneca, <u>Letters</u>. Seneca is the foremost figure of "Stoicism," a practical philosophy aimed directly and exclusively helping us learn to be satisfied within ourselves, to be content in any condition or environment, and to appreciate the full spectrum of our lives. His "Letters" are written to an ambitious adolescent protégé of his that may remind you of yourself.

» Marcus Aurelius, <u>Meditations</u>. Another great Stoic and emperor of Rome, Marcus Aurelius gives us very direct advice on how one lives a great and satisfying life, in particular trying to balance incredible ambition and daily appreciation of experience. This text is sometimes called "The Emperor's Handbook."

» Tim Ferris, <u>The 4-Hour Work Week</u>. Ferris' book broke the back of any justification of blindly running the office rat race. Much of this text is spent on how to specifically liberate oneself from said rat race, but he spends the latter portion of the book discussing how one turns a terrifying situation of infinite options into a satisfying life.

» David Deida, <u>The Way of the Superior Man</u>. Deida brings us a controversial and deeply moving treatise on all aspects of being a man (specifically a masculine character). This includes how to relate to women, but I got the most out of his approach to embracing the inevitability of our own deaths and turning that into a motivation to find our "deepest purpose" and "share our greatest gifts with the world." I suggest the audiobook in particular—he passionately delivers the whole work himself.

» The Dalai Lama, <u>The Art of Happiness</u>. The most abstract of the works I'll suggest, the Dalai Lama focuses on cultivating human relationships and internal states of mind that do more to promote our own happiness and satisfaction than the material states that we're chasing.

On Willpower and Focus: I am not as much of an expert in these fields as I am in eliminating waste. There's been a lot of very good psychology aimed at dramatically improving our current understanding of how our brains handle motivation, addiction, habit, and focus. Being able to start doing something and keep on doing it are perennial challenges for the modern student. The books below provide a great explanation and advice on aligning one's behavior with one's more enlightened motivations.

» Kelly McGonagall, <u>The Willpower Instinct</u>. I think this is the pinnacle of both understanding why (both chemically and psychologically) we don't always act in the ways we wish we would, and how to successfully make changes to our habits. McGonagall is hugely empowering and relieving: she helps us to forgive ourselves without excusing ourselves, and to see our willpower challenges more accurately as states of reality that can be improved with dispassionate analysis and good strategy—rather than personal weaknesses that are best solved with guilt and self-ridicule.

» Chip Heath, <u>Switch</u>. Subtitled "How to Change When Change is Hard," it speaks about how to "flip the switch" between one behavior and another, such that the new behavior becomes the default habit for our brains. The suggestions are highly prescriptive with a "step-by-step" style.

» Jon Kabat-Zinn, <u>Mindfulness for Beginners</u>. A no-preaching, no-religion approach to mindfulness from a doctor whose life has been devoted to helping people overcome psychological and emotional challenges from smoking to depression and PTSD. The audiobook is very accessible and produced quick results for me for improving attentiveness and focus.

» Byron Brown, <u>Soul Without Shame</u>. For many people, habits are reinforced by fear and self-judgment. This judgment often causes us to give up early or to feel so bad that we indulge in the very habits we're trying to change in order to find relief. If failure causes negative self-talk and either giving up or beating up for you, this book is the path to a dispassionate (and ultimately self-loving) approach to the judge inside you that gets in the way of not only taking on tough challenges but simply being happy.

About the Author

Erik Fogg is, as of 2013, an operations and management consultant with Stroud Consulting. He attended MIT for his undergraduate and graduate university and loved every minute. He currently lives in Boston, Massachusetts.

30474044R10071

Made in the USA
San Bernardino, CA
15 February 2016